So you WANT to be a Work-AT-HoME Mom

A CHRISTIAN'S
GUIDE
STARTIN
HOME-BA
BUSINES

D1256548

JILL HART
& DIANA ENNEN

BEACON HILL PRESS
OF KANSAS CITY

Copyright 2009
by Jill Hart, Diana Ennen, and Beacon Hill Press of Kansas City

ISBN 978-0-8341-2466-0

Printed in the
United States of America

Cover Art: Brandon Hill
Interior Design: Sharon Page

Library of Congress Cataloging-in-Publication Data

Hart, Jill.
    So you want to be a work-at-home mom : a Christian's guide to starting a home-based
business / Jill Hart and Diana Ennen.
        p. cm.
    ISBN 978-0-8341-2466-0 (pbk.)
    1. Stay-at-home mothers. 2. Working mothers. 3. Working mothers—Religious
life. 4. Self-employed women. 5. Home-based businesses. 6. Married women—
Employment. 7. Work and family. I. Ennen, Diana. II. Title.
    HQ759.46.H38 2009
    658.1'1412—dc22

                                                                2009026483

10 9 8 7 6 5 4 3 2 1

CONTENTS

FOREWORD

I have great news for those starting on the work-at-home journey. You're not alone on your quest to start a home-based business. Reading books such as this on the topic of working at home, plus partnering together with other Christian work-at-home moms, is a great way to achieve your goals and create a successful business.

I, too, know the struggles of being an entrepreneur. My company, Apronique, continues to be a work in progress. As such, we're still on the "roller-coaster" of exhilaration and deep disappointment. Although I know that God has directed this process, my human nature questions when things don't go as expected. Some time spent with the Word of God, whether in private Bible study or listening to a sermon, fortunately helps with the attitude adjustment. We're then ready to keep going.

There have been times when I wondered if we had come to the end of our journey; and if so, I knew that it had not been in vain. I asked God for direction at those times. His answers are always just in time and completely amazing.

My faith in God has played a huge part in my success. I think life is a progression, and I've been on a journey. From growing up to all those amazing first times, I truly felt God's hand in my life, especially with His leading me into music. He's always been with me. I've always relied strongly on my faith and try to pursue that as wholeheartedly as possible.

It's important to have dreams and visions you want to accomplish. I know I'm a big dreamer. Sometimes dreams might seem out of reach, but they're possible. For example, my recording career has become more than I ever imagined. It's hard to believe that ZOEgirl was together over seven years and that I've now released a solo album and am working with a new group, COLMANblue.

We were especially proud of ZOEgirl as we have numerous songs that God has used to reach out to today's youth. It's been so powerful and wonderful to be a part of that. I think females in particular face so much pressure these days on so many different levels, and music has been an amazing outlet for us to communicate and offer whatever bit of advice we can. We can all relate with the struggles that I think most girls face at some point, including self-worth, self-esteem, and other things like that. Yet it's great to know we aren't alone.

I'm not a very business-minded person by nature, but I've learned a lot through the process of starting my business and my music. I've found it takes a lot of hard work and dedication. Plus, you have to be absolutely committed. With my home-based business, I've been blessed to be working with a business partner who is very dedicated. She's good at so many things, and we complement each other by adding our strengths and supporting the other in areas we're weak in. That's what makes our business work.

For example, she's very good at research, which I feel is the key if you're going to market a product. You need to know what your product is and who your target audience is. It takes a lot of forethought, planning, and dedication, but it's possible.

I always say that if you have an idea and you want a business, just go for it. Know that there are going to be disappointments. We've had several, but God has opened so many wonderful doors for us. We keep praying. We keep seeking Him. We keep our heads up and keep on going. Just stay focused, leave it in God's hands, and let Him guide and direct you.

Let me tell you a little about the business that God has brought into my life, Apronique. We make designer aprons. My business partner, Marilyn Brown, is a wonderful lady and good friend (I actually went to high school with her daughter Rochelle). She's an accomplished seamstress, very much a visionary, and is always looking for new creative outlets.

One day she was reading a magazine that stated that aprons were one of the biggest things going today. She realized that with the big rise in home improvement and cooking shows, and with more people becoming health conscious, this was a very big market. This started her thinking about the aprons of today and also those of the past. It stirred memories she shared with her mother and grandmother cooking and enjoying time together. Yet the photos in the magazine didn't appeal to her, or for that matter, to most of the women of today—especially the younger generation. She realized she could design and create an apron that would have a greater appeal to the fashion-conscious woman.

So we created a new generation of aprons. They reflect current colors, style, trends, and design without looking like the apron Grandma wore. That was it. A magazine sparked a vision, a dream.

Marilyn wanted a partner to help with marketing and designing. She also knew she could succeed better with a popular face. She knew that I had been involved with ZOEgirl and had gone to school with her daughter. So she asked me if I would be interested in partnering with her on Apronique.

It was a perfect time for me, because I was transitioning. We had just moved, and I was already thinking of starting some type of home business. I've had a dream of owning a business, so I was at a good place to consider her offer. I've always loved crafty kinds of things. In fact, I went through a time when I was making and selling scarves while I was on the road. I was involved with crocheting and knitting, so when she came to me with this business idea, I thought it sounded like something that could be fun and a creative outlet for me as well.

That's how my business came to be. The more I work to move Apronique forward, the more I realize that God has orchestrated my life "for such a time as this."

Our tips to new business owners:

- Make certain that God is providing your direction; then try not to waver in your trust of Him. Many situations will arise to test that trust. Remember that just because your steps are ordered by God, that does not guarantee every step you take will miraculously fall into place.

- Use wisdom. Spend wisely.

- Recognize that you truly must be a jack-of-all-trades. We're the seamstress, bookkeeper, supplier locator, mail/shipping clerk, presser, packager, customer service rep, promotional literature creator, webmaster, sales rep, telemarketer, computer expert, debt collector, display creator, advertising executive—and more.

- Research, research, research. It's so much easier now with the Internet. Learn how to successfully conduct online searches.
- Find professionals with whom you can trade services.
- Finally, remember that your business is only a small part of your life (one of my most difficult challenges).

Most important, keep the joy and happiness in your business, and remember it for what it is—a gift from God.

Blessings in Christ,
Kristin Schweain
Apronique.com

Kristin Schweain is a recording artist with the contemporary Christian band COL-MAN*blue, formerly with* ZOE*girl.*

INTRODUCTION

I was miserable and tearful as I drove to work for the first time in more than three years. *Lord, I don't know if I can do this—please give me the strength,* I prayed aloud as I turned into the parking lot of one of the biggest companies in town.

I had left our two-year-old daughter at home with a babysitter just ten minutes earlier and driven the mile or so to my new job with a sense of dread and anticipation. There were so many questions: *What if I don't fit in? What if I can't keep up? What if I burst into tears in the first five minutes?*

I opened the door, gave my name to the receptionist, and took a seat to wait for training to begin. As I looked around, I began to feel a little more at ease. Other new employees waited with me. Some even looked as if they might be moms. Some looked as if they were as nervous as I felt. *I wonder if they had to leave a child at home,* I thought. *Maybe I'm not the only stay-at-home mom headed unwillingly back into the corporate world.*

My life had been going just as planned since I met my husband, Allen. Get married, have kids, stay at home, and raise them—that was exactly how I envisioned things going. Allen was in the Air Force, so I thought I had created a pretty safe haven—one that wouldn't come crashing down around me. One word changed it all.

Korea.

Everything changed. My husband's military career was at a place where he would have to transfer overseas in order to advance. He was willing to do that as long as he was able to bring me and our daughter along. However, the military had other plans. They gave him orders to Korea, a country where only service members are allowed. In a gallant effort to put his family first, Allen decided to request a discharge from the military rather than go overseas without us. I was thrilled. I couldn't have asked for a better husband.

We had a year or so to adjust to the fact that Allen would be leaving the military. He began applying for jobs in his career field, information technology, but the market was swamped, and jobs were few and far between. As the year drew to a close, Allen took the only job he could find, and it paid half of what he had earned in the military.

What would we do? Allen wanted to continue searching for jobs, so asking him to add a second low-paying job seemed out of the question.

I would have to go back to work full time.

I tried to put on a brave face, but I was devastated. My perfect world was crumbling, and I was angry—angry with God, angry with Allen, angry even with myself for being angry. I considered the drastic change this would be in my life: nine-to-five jobs for both of us—and still barely enough money to make ends meet.

Thinking there was no other choice, I buckled down, found a job, and began my new life as a working mom.

During this time I did some real soul-searching. I knew I had to find a way to let go of my anger. It was affecting every relationship in my life, and I was miserable by the time I got home from work, so miserable that I didn't have much left to give to our daughter during the short evenings that I had with her. I knew it couldn't continue.

One day as I was pouring my working-woman woes out to Allen, he asked me something that got me thinking. "Jill," he said, "why have you given up? Maybe working full time is a temporary situation, and you're spending all your time focused on how angry you are instead of how you can alter the situation."

I began praying about what Allen had said, asking the Lord what His plan for my life was. After a few weeks of earnest praying about my situation, I was able to begin letting go of the bitterness that had invaded my heart. I told God that I was ready to accept whatever His plans for me were, even if that meant working full time.

My heart was lighter, and I began thinking about how many other moms must feel the way I had been feeling. I started focusing on a web site I had been developing to help other Christian moms find ways to work from home and be able to raise their families. It was amazing how my attitude did a U-turn once I accepted what God had in store for me and began focusing first on Him and then on others instead of only on myself.

Only two months after that first terrifying day at my new job, I came across an ad in our local newspaper for a work-at-home position. I began working for this business part-time a few evenings a week. A couple of weeks later, Allen landed a great job making more than he had when he was in the military.

I was able to quit my full-time job, work from home, and be at home with our little girl again.

God took us down a long, winding road but had graciously taken us full circle. We now have two beautiful children that I raise full time while running my own business.

—Jill Hart

1 MAKING THE CHOICE TO STAY HOME

Our society is changing. More and more women are leaving the workplace to be stay-at-home moms so they can be more active in their children's lives. They want to be there for first smiles and first steps, and they want to kiss away the boo-boos and wipe away the tears.

Today's moms are passionate women who want both careers and families without having to give up precious time with their children. They're searching for ways to have it all, and they're finding that it's possible to work from home and at the same time balance a family.

It may sound like a dream, but it's not. It does start with a dream, though.

A few fortunate women fall into a job or business that allows them to work at home, but it isn't that easy for most women. To find a way to stay at home while still contributing to their family financially is something that many women long for but few know how to achieve. We hope to make it easier for you.

Being Content at Home

You might have expected us to immediately launch into a chapter about how wonderful life can be if you work at home. However, with the authors having worked from home many years, we realized that you first need to be content in your home life to make it work. The focus of your mind is where true happiness lies. "Where your treasure is, there your heart will be also" (Matthew 6:21).

Before beginning your search for a career that will allow you to work from home, it's important to remember that God has put you where you are for a reason. It may be for a season of your life, or it could possibly be long-term. Either way, trust that God will provide what's best for you, and that may look a little different than what you think is best.

Being a mom and working outside the home can be incredibly challenging. Coordinating schedules, running kids to and fro, and being so tired by evening that you don't have the energy to enjoy your kids take their toll. However, being a work-at-home mom every day, all day, presents its own unique challenges. It can become monotonous, even tedious. The kids, the house, the responsibilities—the list goes on and on. In either case, it can feel downright impossible to have an attitude of gratitude. The road can be hard, but in the end, your life will be less stressful and more satisfying if you can overcome discontentment. Following are some ideas for building contentment.

Be Grateful

One of the hardest attitudes to achieve is that of gratefulness. It's easy to get caught up in the negatives that happen each day. However, it's important to be grateful for each and every blessing that God gives.

Make a list of things in your life that you're grateful for. You can start your list with your family and the opportunity to work from home, and continue from there. Take the time to thank God for each of the things on your list. As you begin to develop a grateful attitude, you'll begin to notice more and more things each day you can add to your list.

Godliness with contentment is great gain. For we brought nothing into the world, and we can take nothing out of it. But if we have food and clothing, we will be content with that (1 Timothy 6:6-8).

17

Give Back

Changing your attitude is the first step to finding contentment. Reaching out and helping others is a proven way to change your attitude. When you extend help and graciousness to others, it can't help but benefit you as well.

Find someone who needs a friend, and make a conscious effort to reach out to him or her every week or every month. Or find a ministry that you admire, and get involved. You'll be surprised what investing something of yourself in others will do for your attitude. If you're running a business from home, you may be able to bless others with a product they can't afford or a special discount that will brighten their day. Maybe you can mentor someone. Be careful, though, that you don't get so involved in helping others that you neglect your own business.

Choose to Accept Your Situation

A key component of contentment is *acceptance.* Acceptance doesn't mean you don't strive to better your life. It simply means that you make peace with where you are in life at this time.

There will always be more to attain—more money, more prestige. If you spend your life focused on what you don't have or what you haven't attained in life, you'll be sad indeed. Celebrate each and every success, no matter how big or how small.

Examine your life and see all that is good in it. Each good thing is a gift from God. Accept that He is with you at this point in time. He'll be with you in every success and every setback. Nothing you do will make Him love you more, and there's nothing you can do that will make Him love you less.

> We are God's workmanship, created in Christ Jesus to do good works, which God prepared in advance for us to do *(Ephesians 2:10).*

Focus on Christ

This may sound like a cliché, but it's easy to allow focus to move from the Lord to self. When moms work at home, the needs of family, business, and self can sometimes be all-consuming, leaving little time to meet spiritual needs. But focusing on your relationship with the Lord is what should come first. If your relationship with Christ is weak, all other relationships will be affected.

Here are practices that will help keep you focused on Him:

1. Read your Bible every day. Make the commitment to read at least one verse every day. The Book of Proverbs is a good place to start, or start with verses from the Gospel of John for a close look at the life of Christ. As you progress to reading more each day, consider purchasing a Bible that will guide you through reading the whole Bible in a year. There are also versions available that will lead you through the Bible in ninety days.

> Do not let this Book of the Law depart from your mouth; meditate on it day and night, so that you may be careful to do everything written in it. Then you will be prosperous and successful *(Joshua 1:8).*

2. Cultivate an active prayer life. You can pray anytime and anywhere—when you're driving, putting on your makeup, cooking, even as you drift off to sleep at night. Take advantage of these precious moments to spend them with your Heavenly Father.

> Be joyful always; pray continually; give thanks in all circumstances, for this is God's will for you in Christ Jesus *(1 Thessalonians 5:16-18).*

3. Meditate on the Word of God. When you find a verse or verses that have deep meaning for you, allow your mind to dwell on them, and let them soak into your spirit. A good starting point might be Romans 8:38-39—"I am convinced that neither death nor life, neither angels nor demons, neither the present nor the future, nor any powers, neither height nor depth, nor anything else in all creation, will be able to separate us from the love of God that is in Christ Jesus our Lord."

Make note of the verses you've chosen, and jot down thoughts or ideas that they bring to mind. Keep your mind focused on Him, and be in prayer that He will open your eyes to what He would have you learn from the verses.

4. Wait. Contentment will not be attained overnight. Feelings of discontentment will push their way in. When they do, look through your life to bring to mind the ways God has changed you, the things He's done to bring you closer to an attitude of contentment. Contentment comes in His timing, so allow Him the time to work in your life.

> Be still before the LORD and wait patiently for him *(Psalm 37:7).*

If the temptation to wallow in discontentment continues to present itself, find someone who will hold you accountable— someone you can trust to be kind but firm who will speak the truth to you lovingly.

When you're feeling dissatisfied or frustrated, give your accountability partner a call, and be honest about your feelings. Every mom gets frustrated; you're certainly not alone. When you find someone you can talk with honestly, it will be an excellent help in overcoming negative thoughts and feelings. Accountability partners know each other on a very real and honest level and still accept and love each other. This allows both of you the opportunity to be supported as well as supportive.

Contentment may seem elusive, but with prayerful deliberation it can be achieved and will bring you more joy and peace than you can imagine. Start working toward an attitude of contentment today.

When your mind and heart are in a good place, it's time to begin thinking about the choices that are available to you. *Can* you work from home? *Should* you work at home? And *how* in the world do you begin your search for success?

Setting Priorities in Business and at Home

Working from home, particularly if you're running your own business, is a time-consuming endeavor—especially for moms. You're responsible not only for the success of the business but for your family as well. You must be self-reliant, self-motivated, and self-disciplined in order to attain success in both areas.

When you work at home, it's easy to let phone calls, e-mail, and paperwork keep you tied down and cause you to feel you don't have time to take a break or choose to spend top-quality time with your family. Maybe you've noticed that you spend more time in front of your computer or on the phone than you expected to when you made the decision to work at home. Maybe you see your kids acting up and trying to get your attention. Maybe the work-at-home dream you envisioned isn't happening.

You started out with noble intentions, but now the excitement of success in your business has caused you to lose sight of the primary reason you chose this path. It happens to many of us who work at home, so don't worry. Help is on the way.

> She considers a field and buys it; out of her earnings she plants a vineyard *(Proverbs 31:16).*

Here are five tips for setting priorities in your life and business:

First, be honest. You probably didn't start your work-at-home career to climb the corporate ladder. Spend some time in prayer, and ask the Lord to show you the things you need to change.

Take a few minutes to answer the following questions about how you've been handling the time commitment of owning a business.

- Are you spending too much time on the phone with clients?
- Do you think about business to the point that you're distracted when you're doing family activities?

- Is television getting more top-quality time with your children than you are?
- Do you snap at your children because of the stresses of your business?

Second, make a list. Sit down and write out a list of things you see that you would like to change. This can be a list of tasks you can do differently, such as limiting the time you spend on your business or ways you can reduce stress so you can deal kindly with your family.

Third, log your time. Buy a notebook or create a spreadsheet to log the time you spend on business. Make a column for each day across the top and a row of half-hour increments down the side. Time yourself every time you sit down at your desk by writing "in" in the box that corresponds to the time and day. Every time you leave your desk or complete a task, write "out" in the appropriate box.

At the end of the week, total up the hours you've spent each day on business tasks. Take special note of how much time you spend on e-mail and things that aren't billable. Are you surprised, or is it about where you thought it would be? This can be a real eye-opener and show you in black and white if your priorities have gotten off track.

Fourth, take a break. If you're in shock after examining your time log, it's time to take a break. If you normally work during the weekend, make it a point to take this weekend off. Shut down your e-mail, turn off the ringer on your business phone, and shut the door to your office.

Plan ahead and schedule your time. Prioritize your workload, and have the work that will require the most effort and concentration scheduled for your peak time. Try not to get sidetracked; stay on task and focus on what you need to do. For example, you'll be amazed by how much more you can accomplish by changing the way you handle e-mail. If you answer it only at scheduled times, you'll find you have more time to do the tasks at hand.

Reevaluate the ways you're spending your time. Try to plan when you can work on your business without losing time with your children. If your children are in school, make it a point to stop working when they get home. If your children are still small, try to plan your time accordingly. Perhaps a babysitter for several hours or days a week is necessary. Another possibility would be to have a grandparent or neighbor watch them once or twice a week to allow you time to work without interruptions.

Fifth, plan an activity. Now that you're ready to make a change in your routine, why not plan an activity once a week? This can be an outing with your children or something simple, like setting aside time to make cookies together. You'll notice that when you plan for these times, they actually happen.

If possible, find another work-at-home mom, and hold one another accountable to keep to your new schedules. Make a weekly play date for your children to spend time together. You and your friend can talk business if necessary, or you may decide to make it a "no business talk allowed" time.

Remember that the years you can work at home and have time with your children are a gift; your business is a gift also. How that will work for you and your family will take a little time to determine and will be different for each family. Take the time to find what works for you, and set your schedule accordingly. Reevaluate your priorities every few months to make sure that you're making the best use of your time. The rewards will be well worth it.

> Sons are a heritage from the Lord, children a reward from him *(Psalm 127:3)*.

2 WHERE TO START

Put simply, running a home-based business means that you're your own boss. What a great feeling! Home-based businesses come in many shapes and forms. You may have started your own company, or you may have joined one of the many home-based businesses available today. For example, you can do publicity or virtual assisting, as Diana does, or you may operate an online community, as Jill does. The possibilities are limitless, and the rewards are great.

Here are Jill's and Diana's stories

Jill's Experience

I began my work-at-home career as a telecommuter. I found my very first telecommuting job through my local newspaper. I was scanning the "Professional/Computers" section of the classifieds, and there it was—the listing I had been dreaming of for months. I can still see it: "Data Entry from Home." I thought it was very likely a scam, so I waited almost a week to talk to my husband about it. I didn't want to get his hopes up—or mine—and then have them dashed when I found out it wasn't for real. The day before I spoke with my husband, I called the number listed in the ad and spoke with one of the hiring managers. I got all the details, verified them through our local Better Business Bureau, and did my best to search online to find any complaints about the company.

Then I brought it up to my husband to see what he would think of the whole idea. We had been married only a few months and didn't have children, so I wasn't sure if he would be open to the idea of my working from home at that point.

I was pleased to find that he was supportive. We decided that before I went as far as quitting my full-time job, I should try to pursue the telecommuting opportunity part-time for a few months.

I applied for the job, interviewed, and started that same month. I worked my full-time job every day, then came home to my new part-time job. It went very well. After about three months of praying about the situation and working both jobs, my husband and I felt this was the path that God was directing us down, and I quit my full-time job. I've never looked back.

During my months of working both jobs, I scoured the Internet looking for a web site that would tell me more about working from home. I wanted to learn more about it and see if there might be a better opportunity—something that better fit my interests and would provide more income. I found a few work-at-home web sites but none that I felt I could trust. I didn't find any sites specifically for Christians. In the back of my mind, I thought a Christian work-at-home site would be great, but I never dreamed I would be the one God would use to begin the community that has become Christian Work at Home Moms (CWAHM).

I created CWAHM.com as a way to practice the new web design skills I was learning from my husband. The site rose quickly in the search engines, because there were no other sites like it specifically targeting Christians. Soon CWAHM was sought after by Christian moms looking for the same information I had been looking for, and it's now become one of the primary Christian work-at-home sites on the Web. My prayer is that God will continue to use it to minister to Christian women to encourage and direct those who want to work from home and to aid those who already work from home.

Diana's Experience

I started working from home in 1985. I had worked as a medical secretary and executive secretary for years. The positions I held carried a lot of responsibility and a lot of hard work, but they were rarely acknowledged. Then, when my son was born, the decision to put him into daycare was just too tough. I didn't want strangers raising him, and like many of you, I longed to be the one who was there for his firsts—first real smile, first crawl, first steps, and all the other firsts.

After a few weeks in daycare and more tears than I want to admit, I convinced my husband to let me type from home. He was a little reluctant at first, but he then agreed it would be the best for us and what he wanted for our family as well. My business was born.

In 1985 the technology was not what it is today. I actually started on a word processor and didn't even own a computer. One day shortly after starting, my first client made a change in a ten-page document that required a complete rewrite. With a computer it would have taken minutes. With my word processor it was two hours of retyping every page. Off to Radio Shack we went, and I purchased my first computer. I was in heaven.

I was extremely fortunate, because my marketing was very effective, and I had a full-time client base almost immediately. Although that was fabulous for me, I hadn't planned for it to happen so quickly. I wasn't prepared for all that work, and I didn't have my bookkeeping set up. And, like many of you moms reading this, I realized that working with a baby at home was a bit more difficult than I had anticipated.

The one thing I did know was that this was what I wanted, and I was going to make it work no matter what. That spirit is what has enabled me to continue to this day. I also felt that this was the direction in which God was leading me. Little did I know back then that I would eventually write books that would help others work at home. God's plan is always so much better than we envision.

Business was going great, and in 1996 I wrote my first book on starting a home-based business. People were always asking me how I did it, so I decided to write *Words from Home: Start, Run and Profit from a Home-Based Word Processing Business.* I wasn't really expecting success, but I wanted to put a tool in the hands of other mothers who wanted to work at home and spend more time with their children. I was on a mission; I knew that if I could do it, others could too.

More books followed, and my business continued to thrive. I can truly say that I have enjoyed the entire journey. Over the years I changed the focus of my business as I learned new skills, and the Internet and technology opened new horizons. In 2001 I met Kelly Poelker online, and we decided to write a book on how to start a Virtual Assistant business. We wrote *Virtual Assistant—The Series: Become a Highly Successful, Sought After VA.* It's still one of my best sellers. And even better, Kelly and I became great friends.

I ran a successful business, raised a family, and pursued a close walk with Christ. Even though I wasn't out in the business world eight hours every workday, I was able to have close, rewarding connections with friends online.

Today I focus primarily on publicity, virtual assistant coaching, and marketing of my books. I cherish the moments when people write me and say, "I'm in business today because of your books." My hope is that the book you're now reading will help others as well.

Follow Your Heart

When God wants something for us, He often leads us in a way that's unique to our situations. Sometimes He has to beat us over the head before we listen, but He's faithful to see us through.

How about you? How many times have you felt that He was speaking to you personally, leading you and telling you the right direction to go or not go? If you feel that God is leading you in the direction of working from home, take steps to ensure that you're moving in the right direction. There are some basic steps you can take to make sure you're in God's will.

Prayer

Seeking Him is always the best and first route we should take. Why is it that many times, especially when making some of life's toughest decisions, God is the last one we turn to? We find ourselves constantly trying to solve our own problems and make our own decisions. Even though the Bible and godly people tell us better, and even though we've seen God move in amazing ways, we always try to take control, don't we? We encourage you not to make this mistake. Seek Him.

Seek first his kingdom and his righteousness, and all these things will be given to you as well *(Matthew 6:33)*.

Seek Godly Counsel

God puts certain people in our lives for a reason. Can you think of two or three people in your life who love the Lord and whom you trust? Explain to them your desire to work from home, and ask their opinions. Ask them to pray for you and with you for God to guide your path and lead you to make a wise decision at the right time for the right reasons.

> Where two or three come together in my name, there am I with them *(Matthew 18:20).*

Wait

The work-at-home world can be fast-paced, and many companies will push you to make a decision quickly. However, Scripture tells us clearly to wait upon the Lord. Seven times in the Book of Psalms (KJV) alone—37:9; 59:9; 62:1; 62:5; 104:27; 123:2; 145:15—we're told to wait upon the Lord. Scripture tends to repeat important lessons. If we find "wait upon the Lord" seven times in just one book of the Bible, it must be important.

> Delight yourself in the LORD and he will give you the desires of your heart *(Psalm 37:4).*

Psalm 37:4 is a well-known verse, but it's interesting to think about where the desires of our hearts come from. Who puts those desires in our hearts?

The desires that God gives us are desires that He placed within us when He created us. Why do some women want to work from home and others love being in the workplace? God has created each of us differently—with different needs and desires.

He knows us far better than we know ourselves. If you long to work from home, seek Him. He'll show you the way to follow your heart.

A Note from Diana

When I started writing this book, I felt His presence and His encouragement to do it. Jill and I both meet challenges in our businesses—challenges that we believe others working from home face. As we were writing this book, we sensed Him giving us direction in what to include. We have shared it with you as best we could.

As you begin your home-based business, do the same. Listen to what He says, and follow the path He gives you. Just as God is always there for you in your personal life, He will be there for you in your business. Listen to your heart. Listen for His guidance. Go forward with the knowledge that He's beside you, helping you on your journey. Trust Him to show you the next step.

Where to Start

The following questions will help you zero in on the best home-based business for you.

1. What type of businesses would you like to hear more about?

2. What type of products are you interested in representing?

3. How much can you invest in starting your own business?

Note: When starting a home-based business, there may be start-up fees for a business kit, web site, or training materials.

4. How many hours a week are you willing or able to devote to your own business?

5. When are you planning to start your business?

6. How much money are you hoping to make each month?

7. What skills and experience do you have that you feel will be beneficial to your business?

Answering these questions will help you think about what will work for you and will help you formulate questions to ask prospective business representatives. If you can find a business or product that you love and are passionate about, it will make running a home-based business much easier. If you love what you do, it shows. If you can wake up each morning and know that you will spend another day doing what you love—taking care of your family and your business—you will be blessed indeed. It *is* possible!

Do your homework before you begin any home-based business or telecommuting position. You must decide if it's right for you.

You must also decide if you'll work on a full-time or part-time basis. Weigh the pros and cons of both, and be honest about the amount of time you can devote to your business while caring for your family. Many women start out part-time to establish their business and then go full-time once they have a firm client base and can bring in the necessary income for them to be at home full-time.

If you haven't already, begin praying today that God will direct you to the perfect business for *you.* No business is perfect, but there may be one that's perfect *for you.* Just as He has provided you with the perfect spouse for you, He will also be faithful to guide you in your business decisions if you wait on Him. God gives us what we need.

After you've answered the seven questions and have started thinking about what type of business you might be interested in, you can start researching what types of home-based business opportunities are available. Keep a list of opportunities that interest you as you come across them.

Telecommuting

"Telecommuting" is a term that confuses many people. Miriam-Webster defines it as simply "To work at home by the use of an electronic linkup with a central office" (<http://www.merriam-webster.com/dictionary/telecommute>).

Telecommuters are hired by a company, often their previous employer, to work from a home office. Some women choose to set up a business, and others choose to seek employment with an outside company that hires at-home workers.

When Jill began working from home, she was employed by a local company as an independent contractor to be a data extractor. Her job was to extract information from résumés that had been submitted to the company she worked for and input that information into a database. She was paid per résumé processed.

As you can imagine, it took a lot of processing to make a decent wage. As she got better at the job, she made more per hour. Each week she received a paycheck from the company, and at the end of the year the company sent her a 1099 form for tax purposes. Jill was a *telecommuter*.

Diana began working at home by starting her own home-based business. She did secretarial work for others and charged them based on the rates that she had set herself. Each client signed a contract with her to perform the work. Diana was a *home-based business owner.*

A telecommuter's employer sets wages and pays regularly. A home-based business owner is responsible for finding clients, setting payment, completing the work, and collecting payment.

Pros and Cons of Telecommuting

Telecommuting can be a rewarding experience. You work from home, bring in a regular income, and usually have the support of a company behind you.

One benefit of a telecommuting job is that it provides a stable income. You know—or at least can predict—the amount of income that will be coming in each month. Also, if you find a company willing to hire you as an employee as opposed to an independent contractor, the employer will take care of your taxes. That can be a major consideration for many people. Some companies even provide benefits to telecommuters.

A telecommuting job also allows you to avoid the stress that goes with running a business. You just do what they tell you to do—no marketing, advertising, or selling to deal with. You do your job, get paid, and hopefully, don't have to think any more about it.

The downside of a telecommuting position may be that your time is not as flexible. Many companies require a regular schedule, set hours, or at least a set number of hours that you'll work. Also, with many types of telecommuting jobs you'll be paid only for the hours you're actually working. In some cases you may spend six hours in front of the computer but be paid for only the four hours your fingers were actually pressing keys.

If you are hoping to find a telecommuting job, you'll need to make sure you're qualified for one of these highly sought positions. Training is available for these types of careers. Getting the training needed for the position you have in mind may give you the edge you need to get a foot in the door.

Pros and Cons to Beginning a Home-Based Business

Pro: Home-based businesses offer a great amount of flexibility, a definite plus for many work-at-home moms. Most of us want to have the income that comes from working as well as the time to spend with our children. Home-based businesses offer this flexibility, because you're your own boss, and that allows you to set your own schedule. The amount you make depends on the amount of effort you put into it.

On the flip side, you can easily take time off when necessary. You're in total control of the hours you work each day, whether you will work full-time or part-time, and how you choose to run your business.

Pro: Being your own boss allows you the freedom to set your own goals. Your success is tied directly to how much of your time, effort, and resources you're willing to put into your business. This may seem overwhelming, but if you're in a business you love, it will be second nature to work hard and achieve the goals you set for yourself. One way to achieve big goals is to set smaller goals and celebrate reaching each one, no matter how small.

Pro: Owning your own business also gives you something to call your own. Being a woman, wife, mom, daughter, or aunt can be overwhelming, and most of us have the desire to have something to be proud of that we're solely responsible for creating. A home-based business is a great way to channel that desire as you create your own success.

Pro: Another rewarding aspect is the creativity that it allows you to express. We don't mean get-out-the-scissors-and-glue creativity, but the creativity that's unleashed when you're running a business you're passionate about. Many aspects of running a home-based business require creativity, such as marketing and networking. Every woman must find the right business for her and express her own creativity in different aspects of the business. That's what makes it so exciting.

Con: When running a home-based business, your income may not be as stable and predictable as it would be if you were an employee—especially as you're establishing your business. It takes time to build a customer base as well as learn the how-to of running a successful business. The good news, though, is that there's a wealth of information available today. Many companies offer training, both online and offline, as well as mentors and leaders to assist you in developing your business and your techniques. If you take advantage of the knowledge of those before you who have already built successful businesses, you may be able to reduce the learning curve.

Con: Another one of the downsides to home-based businesses is the bookkeeping. You must be careful to keep track of not only your income but also your expenses. It's imperative to keep good records and know what type of income your business is bringing in. If your business grows more than expected, you might be surprised at tax time.

It takes time and effort to run a successful home-based business. On the flip side, it can be exhilarating, and the freedom it allows you makes up for what you're putting into it.

Hobby vs. Business

When beginning a home-based business, it's important to remind yourself that to make a profit you must treat it like work, not play. Running a business is hard work, and it takes perseverance and determination. If you approach your business as a hobby that happens to make you a little money, it will probably never be anything more than that.

In order to succeed, you must set attainable goals and strive to reach them. You'll need to follow up with your customers, provide customer service, and balance this with family life. Once you take it to this level, the product or service you once loved to do as a hobby may not seem so worthwhile.

We encourage you to take a deep look at your commitment level at this step in your decision-making process. Ask yourself if the business you're considering is something you see yourself working on in five years. What about ten? If the answer is no, reconsider which home-based career will be right for you.

3 CHOOSING THE RIGHT BUSINESS FOR YOU

With home-based businesses estimated to be a $427 billion-a-year industry, according to *Entrepreneur* magazine, you can see the great potential of working at home. Plus, with fluctuating gas prices, the high cost of childcare, and the desire to be in charge of your financial future, more and more people are choosing to come home from corporate America every day. Whatever the individual reasons are, there's one word that sums it up: freedom.

Numerous types of home-based businesses are available today. We'll explain several of them and provide tips from moms who run these types of businesses. Also, in the back of this book are profiles of a few Christian work-at-home moms. Do your research before starting any type of business. We don't personally endorse all the companies listed but instead wanted to provide you with types of businesses available.

Virtual Community Leader

Building and growing an online community is much harder than it looks. Jill began CWAHM in 2000 as a place to compile her research on work-at-home opportunities. The growth of the CWAHM community since its humble beginnings can truly be attributed to the Lord. Jill began with very little knowledge of web design and no online presence whatsoever. Yet despite the odds, the little community took on a life of its own, and after only a few months Jill began receiving e-mail from moms asking how they might get involved.

An online community usually consists of a web site packed full of information. The site is generally the focal point of the community. The exchanging of ideas and building of relationships, however, occurs through message boards, newsletters, blogs, and other interactive resources.

CWAHM, for instance, provides job listings, business listings, classified ads, spiritual encouragement, information, and offers for Christians who want to work from home. We strive to provide spiritual encouragement as well as work-at-home resources. The web site is designed to help moms—and dads—find and request information regarding telecommuting jobs, home businesses, and other information of special interest to Christian parents.

CWAHM.com also strives to produce a network of Christians who work from home and help each other achieve that goal. The goal of CWAHM.com is to help readers make contact with and have ready access to organizations and resources that will help them be more informed and more successful.

Virtual Assistants

As noted earlier, Diana is a virtual assistant and has written numerous books on starting a virtual assistant (VA) business. She's thrilled to see where the VA Industry is today and sees only more amazing things happening as word spreads about all the great things a VA can do. In fact, virtual assistants have been featured on the *Today Show* and *CBS News*, in the *Wall Street Journal*, *Reader's Digest*, *Entrepreneur* magazine, *Woman's World*, *Woman's Day*, and many more. Many businesses say they can't function without virtual assistants, because they're able to do ten times more with the creativity and organizational skills of the VA.

What exactly is a virtual assistant? As quoted in *Virtual Assistant—The Series: Become a Highly Successful, Sought-After VA,*

> A virtual assistant, or VA, is a highly skilled professional who provides administrative support and other specialized services to businesses, entrepreneurs, executives, sales professionals, and others who have more work to do than time to do it.

VAs work as independent contractors, most from their homes, some from outside their homes. VAs use leading-edge technology to communicate work assignments via the Internet, e-mail, disk transfer, or traditional methods like regular mail, overnight shipping, and even pick-up and delivery in local areas. A VA's services typically include Internet research, word processing, medical or legal transcription, database management, handling e-mail, reminder service, bulk mailings, information processing, and any other tasks typically given to the office secretary. Many VAs also provide web development, design and maintenance, meeting and event planning, desktop publishing, bookkeeping, and business start-up consultations. The services are endless, depending upon the VA's knowledge, skills, and creativity.

A few other tasks that a VA can do include—

- book marketing and publicity
- administrative duties
- medical, legal, and general transcription
- bookkeeping
- web design
- real estate assistance
- article and press release distribution
- social networking updates
- business start-up consultations
- editing and proofing
- customizing a shopping cart or autoresponder
- travel arrangements

Virtual assistants provide many services for their clients and often specialize in working with a specific type of business or industry, commonly referred to as *developing a niche*. We have profiled two virtual assistants in the final chapter of this book to provide their personal experiences and tips.

Medical Transcription

Many of us have heard of medical transcriptionists, but few know what it is that they do. *The American Heritage Medical Dictionary* defines a medical transcriptionist as "a person who transcribes medical reports dictated by a physician concerning a patient's health care."

Margery Hinman, director of the MT Advantage Career Center, provides the following information:

Medical transcription is one of today's most lucrative work-at-home businesses. With the inception of the Internet and the ease of receiving and sending reports back and forth via digital encrypted e-mail, transcription services and doctors from across the country are hiring transcriptionists who work from their homes transcribing doctors' medical reports. Because digital dictation is easier, faster, and cheaper than the old cassette tape/transcriber system, more and more companies are switching to digital systems.

As a medical transcriptionist, it is important to understand how digital dictation works. Employers want to hire computer-literate MTs. In addition to learning the technology, it is also important to have a thorough background in subjects such as anatomy and physiology, medical terminology disease processes, laboratory and pathology, pharmacology, diagnostics, and computers. Once you've learned those subjects, you then train your ear to hear by putting them to use in practice dictation.

When looking for an MT school, it's important to have instructors who are certified and who give one-on-one feedback. Make sure your school offers job placement services for its graduates, and make sure it offers plenty of computer instruction (<www.mtacc.net>).

Freelance Writing

Freelancing opportunities are also available for writing and editing as well. For example, many women who work at home write press releases, articles, web copy, and even books for a living. Writing can be done from the convenience of your home, and with the Internet, availability of ebooks, and the ease of publicity today, you can make a great profit as well.

Following is a short interview with Christian author Kathleen Y'Barbo at <www.kathleenybarbo.com>:

Q. Tell us about your business.

A. I am the author of more than thirty novels and novellas geared for the Christian market.

Q. How did you decide on your business?

A. I started as a voracious reader, though I always liked writing. Eventually I decided to try writing a novel.

Q. What are some requirements of starting a writing career?

A. A knowledge of grammar and punctuation and a willingness to learn the skills required to write.

Q. Name the one thing you love best about your business.

A. Easy—I get paid to make up stories!

Q. Give us tips on what makes you successful.

A. I bought books with instructions on developing writing skills and found a writers' group in my area.

Q. How do you market your business?

A. The publishing house does that through their marketing department, and usually an outside publicist schedules interviews and blog tours. I also do book signings and other events to make the public aware of the book I have coming out next.

Q. What is the biggest lesson you've learned?

A. Never stop trying to improve your writing skills. No matter how much you know, you're never going to know it all.

Q. What tip would you give to someone who wants to start a business?

A. Do your homework, and be honest with yourself as to how much time and energy you will put into the business. A writer is essentially never away from the office, because anything can be used as fodder for a book.

Q. How do you balance work and family?

A. My children are grown now, but when they were little I wrote while they were either at school or sleeping. I now have a laptop that I bring with me into the den when the family is watching a movie.

Q. Anything else?

A. Seek what your purpose is, and God will show you.

Inventor—Creating a New Product

Have you always envisioned taking your idea and making it into a product and selling it? That's what Leslie Haywood did. Leslie is the founder of Charmed Life Products and the inventor of Grill Charms (<www.grillcharms.com>). Following is an interview with Leslie in which she tells us about starting her own business.

Q. Tell us about your business.

A. I invented Grill Charms. Grill Charms are the size of a dime with a decorative head and a stem that is textured so the charm won't fall out of the food during grilling. The charms are made of food-grade solid stainless steel and sit flush on the food so they won't catch on the grill when being moved or flipped. Food is Grill Charmed prior to cooking so when it comes off the grill, perfectly charred and plated, each guest can recognize his or her special order by the Grill Charm.

Q. How did you decide on your business?

A. One evening in April 2006, my husband was grilling some fantastic boneless chicken breasts for friends and family. The flavor of the evening was jerk, which we all love. Some people happen to like their chicken "jerkier" than others—some of us like ours on the milder side. When all the chicken came off the grill and was arranged on a serving plate, brought upstairs, and served, my husband couldn't tell which chicken was spicy. Wouldn't you know it, me being a "mild" person, I bit right into the hottest one of all! My husband said "I wish there was a way to tell which chicken was which." Immediately I knew we had something; it was a light-bulb moment. I started sketching prototypes that night and never looked back.

Q. What was required to start your business?

A. A little money, a *lot* of passion and drive, patience, and support from friends and family. It doesn't hurt to be a little nuts. The rest just falls into place if you do your homework.

Q. How did you find out about the legalities for your business?

A. Through wonderful free resources like the Small Business Administration (SBA), Small Business Development Centers (SBDC), and Service Corps of Retired Executives (SCORE).

Q. Name the thing you love best about your business.

A. I love logging onto the computer never knowing what's waiting for me. It's such a thrill to open my inbox—*Did I land that big account? Is there another order? Did someone I admire request a sample?* It's like Christmas every morning.

Q. Give us tips on what makes you successful.

A. Now if I knew that, I'd take my show on the road and make billions! Seriously, the short answer is that nobody told me I couldn't succeed. And even if they had, I wouldn't have listened. I worked for corporate America until the birth of our first daughter, then left a fantastic company and wonderful career in sales to be a stay-at-home mom. Being a mother is the hardest thing I have ever done. I have a head for business, a heart for sales, and like most mothers, can multi-task as if I had four eyes, two heads, and eighteen arms. I've nursed an infant while potty training a two-year-old while talking on the phone as I sautéed mushrooms on the stove with a roast in the oven and two loads of laundry going. I am a fighter and a survivor, and I do not take no for an answer.

Q. How do you market your business?

A. Both wholesale and online.

Q. What is the biggest lesson you've learned?

A. It's really important to get out there well before you have your product. Create the buzz, talk to people in your field, and do lots of networking well in advance of your launch. When you already have a group of people who know you and your story, when the time comes to sell your product or open your business, these are the people who will have known you way back when and will be willing to help you succeed. It truly takes a village. Early on in the process I started recruiting mine. I would not be where I am without their support, which they gave long before I launched my product.

Q. What tip would you give to those wishing to start a business?

A. Expect the unexpected, and never give up. At various times I had to go back to the drawing board. I had done a lot of research on various metal processes, so I had in my head that I needed a specific process—investment casting. This was proving to be too expensive, so I had to start over. Also, the original design of the stem at one point had to be reworked because there was a breakage problem. There was also a time when I thought I had picked the wrong material and should have gone with another metal entirely! I'm learning that it's pretty common in the inventing world to have to scrap what you initially thought was the perfect process, material, or design and just start fresh. Don't let setbacks discourage you; it's all just part of the journey. You'll run into roadblocks, and there will be people and circumstances that will try to keep you down. Keep going. You're in control of how this crazy entrepreneurial story goes. Don't give the pen to another author. Stay in control, stay focused, and when plans A, B, C, and D fall through, E, F, and G will be there if you know where to look.

Q. How do you balance work and family?

A. It's a balancing act that is perpetually out of balance. I try my hardest to make sure the kids don't pay the price of having an entrepreneur for a mom, but I'm also not kidding myself. They watch a little more TV than I'd like, and there have been days I have snapped at them when they didn't deserve it because the stress of doing both just broke me down. But I really make a concerted effort to do both and do both well. By the same token, to some degree, my business pays a price because I'm a mom. For example, not too long ago my five-year-old was very sick, and the marketing efforts I had mapped out for that week had to be put on hold. My house sometimes is a total and complete disaster. The stuff that needs to get done around the house just doesn't get done. Nobody can do it all! My kids come first, my husband comes next, and thankfully he requires very little. My business comes third, and that eats up every other ounce of time and energy I have. Sometimes the dust bunnies are taking over, the plants are dead, the hot tub is green, and the shower is black.

Q. Anything else?

A. I'm just an average mom, with average intelligence, with an average idea, with above-average heart, above-average dreams, and above-average vision. If I can take a crazy idea and turn it into a successful business, anyone can!

Multilevel Marketing

Multilevel marketing (MLM), also known as network marketing, is a system of marketing products through a network of sales representatives or distributors. The standard multilevel marketing program works through recruitment of new representatives. Once a person chooses to become a representative with an MLM company, he or she will earn money, not only through sales of the company's products and through recruiting other representatives, but also by receiving a portion of the income of the representatives he or she has signed up to come into the company. By contrast, in single-level marketing the consultants, distributors, representatives, and so forth make money by buying products from a parent company and selling them directly to customers.

Direct Sales

Direct sales can best be defined by going online to the Direct Selling Association at <www.dsa.org>:

> Direct selling is the sale of a consumer product or service, person-to-person, away from a fixed location. These products and services are marketed to customers by independent salespeople. Depending on the company, the salespeople may be called distributors, representatives, consultants or various other titles. Products are sold primarily through in-home product demonstrations, parties and one-on-one selling.

A direct sales company allows you to purchase products from them at wholesale prices and resell these goods to consumers through home parties, catalogs, or a web site. Some of these companies require that you keep a small inventory of their products on hand while others allow you to place the order and have the products delivered directly to the consumer. Representatives of these companies make money directly through the sales of products.

Some of the benefits of direct selling include the following:

- You choose the hours and the number of hours you work.
- In direct sales the sky's the limit, meaning that a high earning potential is reachable.
- Direct selling companies usually provide consultants, distributors, representatives, general training guides, promotional materials, commission reports, and sales tracking.
- Specifically designed to be a home-based business, direct sales is often the business choice of women and mothers.

Online parties are a big thing today, and people can make a great number of connections through them. In addition, those sponsoring contests can increase awareness of their businesses.

> She watches over the affairs of her household and does not eat the bread of idleness *(Proverbs 31:27).*

There are many direct sales companies. Following is some information about just a few of them furnished to us by women who have their own direct sales business.

Noah's Ark Animal Workshop

Noah's Ark Animal Workshop is a traveling stuffed animal workshop that gives kids the opportunity to make their own hand-stuffed, adorable collectables. We also launched a sister workshop called Bella Bee Workshop, which is a virtue-based traveling glamour-girl workshop that emphasizes friendship, truth, and kindness while having fun with lip gloss, nail polish, body sprays, and fashion accessories.

Many home businesses in my area are geared toward women, and when this opportunity came along, it seemed like the perfect fit. I'm able to work with children, involve my own family in my events, and exercise my entrepreneurial spirit.

This is a service-oriented, home-based business that does not rely on home parties. Fortunately, the kid's market is full of opportunities. I've conducted workshops at birthday parties, group homes, hospitals, schools, day care centers, and corporate parties, and have enjoyed working numerous community events. There are no limits.

Here are my tips for starting a home business:

- Choose your business carefully. It's important to represent a company you're proud to be associated with and committed to.

- Persevere. There will be times when you can't work your business as much as you would like because of other priorities, and there will be periods when you can devote more attention to it. It's important to give yourself a chance to build your customer base and gain a good reputation. Be attentive to your customers, and be in touch with them at least quarterly.

—Ann Campbell
Noah's Ark Animal Workshop

AngelArts

Discover your callings. Before choosing a business to pursue at home, spend time with the Lord. Here are some questions to ask Him.

What have you called me to do and be in this life?

How have you gifted me?

What is my mission in life?

How can I be part of your plan of redemption in my business, my personal life, and my family?

What spiritual gifts have you given me?

What are my values?

What am I passionate about?

What is your/my vision for my life?

Pray, journal, and read Scripture. 2 Corinthians is a great place to start on this journey. Keep praying, and answers will come until they're developed into a fine-tuned mission and vision statement.

Major corporations spend a lot of time on mission statements. Why not Christians who want to start a home business? Then as opportunities arrive, you have a guideline to follow.

—Dana Susan Beasley

<www.angelartswebstore.com>

Southern Living at Home

Southern Living at Home is a home-décor company. I got into the business expecting to have fun, meet new friends, and get amazing products. Here I am four years later, and God has shown He had a different plan for me. I've met many wonderful people and work with an amazing team. In four years our team has grown to 400 women.

I've been blessed through direct sales to have more time with my family, increased self-confidence, and new and lasting friendships. And in addition to all that, I get paid!

—Tammy Degenhart
<www.southernlivingathome.com>

Avon

I started my Avon business several years ago. My business has grown much larger that I expected, and I have had more fun then I ever dreamed possible.

Most of my business, probably ninety percent, comes from face-to-face contact with my customers. I've had goals for my Avon business from the beginning, and those goals have served me well. My current ones are to increase my online presence and build my team through recruiting.

I have great respect for the company I represent, I love the products, and I take pleasure in bringing my customers top-quality products at affordable prices. I feel I'm exactly where God wants me to be, and I thank Him for that.

My home-based business has given me the opportunity to give to my family, my church, and my community.

—Cecilia Frederick

4 SETTING UP YOUR HOME-BASED BUSINESS

When setting up your home office, there are many things that you'll want to take into consideration. First, where will you set up your office? You can set it up somewhere as simple as your kitchen table, but that may not be the best use of space. Think salad dressing on your paperwork. Granted, flexibility is one of your motivations for working from home, but as soon as it's feasible, you'll need to set up a place somewhere in your home that will make you feel like the professional you are.

Imagine this: You've just started your new business as a virtual assistant, and you've landed your first client. The client drops by to meet you, give you the initial paperwork, and sign the payment retainer. You meet her at the front door in shorts and a wrinkled t-shirt. As she steps in, you motion her into your kitchen. As you're clearing off a space on the table to set your laptop, you knock over your morning cereal. Luckily, Sparky, the family dog, is close at hand and begins lapping up the milk and mushy cereal remains.

Get the idea? This example is somewhat extreme, but you would be surprised what some people think are acceptable business practices when they work from home.

A much better approach is to answer the door in a business-casual outfit—for example, khaki pants and a cotton shirt. You welcome your new client and show her the way to your home office, which may be a desk and filing cabinet in the corner of the basement, but you've organized it so that it gives a much more professional appearance than a laptop on the kitchen table. The family dog is shut away in another room, and the remains of breakfast are in the kitchen, not the workspace.

When choosing a workspace, consider whether or not you'll have clients coming to your home. If you will, you'll want to make sure that you have a place—no matter how small—set aside to meet with them.

If you're hoping to claim your office as a tax deduction, you'll need to make sure that you have a separate room that's not used for any other purpose. Check with your tax professional on any other regulations that must be followed to claim this deduction.

Diana has now converted the entire family room into an office. Because she needs lots of "proofing room," she bought two desks with black glass tops and set them in an L-shape in the corner of the office. She works at one desk, and the other is for books, proofing, and spreading out material. She also has a third desk that's used by her daughter after school for computer games or by her assistant during the day.

One item Diana considers a necessity for her home office is a television set. The kids can be close to Mom and watch TV while she works, and if she has to work in the evening, she can catch her favorite shows and still get some work done. It doesn't feel so much like working when she can be productive and watch TV.

On the other hand, there are many benefits to setting your home office in a separate room in a separate part of the house. It will be much easier for you to leave your work at work. Jill finds it easier to concentrate in a separate workspace where there are fewer interruptions. Even though her son is small, he's learned that when Mommy is at the computer, she's working.

If you don't have a separate room to turn into an office, it's still possible to make yourself an office space. Find a corner or section of a room that you can use to set up a desk, a filing cabinet, and whatever else you'll need. Try to make the space in some way distinct from the rest of the room.

Diana and Jill each started out using an extra room as an office. After babies, though, their offices became nurseries. Diana now uses the family room as an office, and Jill has an extra room she uses as an office in the new house they bought a few years ago.

You may need to get creative about where to put an office if you have limited space. However, don't give up. There are

SETTING UP YOUR HOME-BASED BUSINESS

probably many spaces in your home that will work for as office. A bedroom, a portion of your basement, the family room, or even an enclosed porch would work nicely. Remember that as your family grows or grows up you might have to move your office. Try to have a backup plan. Using the kitchen table might seem easy to start, but how will you keep your business organized if all your work is in a pile on the table?

You would be amazed at some of the spaces that have been converted into workable office spaces. In fact, even a closet works. In her column that appeared in the *Washington Post* on February 17, 2006, Heloise advised readers to look for nooks and crannies that could serve as an office. She said a standard size or walk-in closet can work by adding a custom-sized desktop, shelves, and electrical outlets. Two filing cabinets and a smooth piece of wood can become a desk. Another of her tips is to hide a corner office with a three-panel screen.

Diana was skeptical until she went to the home of a woman who was starting a new home-based business and found she had her office set up in a large closet right off of the living room, and it's working just fine for now.

Another businesswoman was able to put a small computer desk in her closet and has a file cabinet to her right and shelves overhead. It's small, but she says she can get everything done that needs to be. One of the greatest features is that she can close the door and leave the office behind.

Computer Setup

One big consideration when setting up an office is where to put the computer. People often don't devote a lot of time and thought to that, and once they have the office all set up, they discover they have a real problem.

Don't set your computer up in a window facing the street. That just invites troubles. No need to advertise your computer and other office electronics.

Glare on your computer screen can be another concern. Diana used to endure a glare that made it almost impossible for her to work for thirty minutes every morning when the sun hit her computer screen. Even closing the blinds didn't eliminate the problem, and she had to eventually rearrange her office.

Also, consider having two computers. It's really not that costly; just don't discard your old computer when you buy a new one. Put the older computer in the living room so you can answer e-mail at night if you want to. Also, consider a laptop that can be moved around.

Business Necessities

Next, you'll need to decide what type of equipment you'll need for your home office. You'll likely need a computer even if your business is not directly online. We would encourage you to make use of the resources available on the Internet today.

Some of the major equipment you might need:

- Desk
- Comfortable, ergonomic chair
- Footrest
- Computer(s)
- Fax machine
- Printer

- Phone—and possibly a separate phone line for your business
- Answering machine or voice-mail service
  Note: Phones today often come with a fax, answering machine, and so forth included. Be sure to check out these options.

Business Supplies

Depending on the type of business or job you'll be doing, you may also need the following supplies:

- Printer supplies
- Pens and pencils
- Paper (lots of it)
- Three-holed paper
- Three-ring binders
- Expandable file
- Paper clips
- Stapler and staples
- File folders
- File cabinet
- Fonts
- Business cards
- Brochures
- Letter- size envelopes
- 9 x 12 envelopes
- 10 x 13 envelopes
- Stamps
- Business phone line (optional)

- Phone headset (optional)
- Internet access (imperative)

Other Essentials:

- Gas money (as you go out to meet prospects or hand out fliers)
- Fees for registering your business
- A business checking account
- Work-related books
- Bookkeeping essentials—books, software, and so on
- Clip art collections
- Software—for web design, word processing, and so on

We suggest making up a list of each and every item you can think of that you'll need. Next, go through and decide the items that are your first priorities and the items that can wait. Start accumulating those you'll need.

Watch for sales throughout the year, and stock up on things you use on a regular basis. For example, back-to-school specials in July and August can be a great cost savings for many of your office needs. You can also find items at that time that aren't available year round.

One of the ways that gets Jill motivated is making an "items that can wait" list and then picking one item from the list and making that a goal. Jill states, "I wanted a fax/printer/copier one year, so my goal was to make and save enough to buy one. I'm happy to say that I did accomplish my goal, but it didn't happen overnight."

Even if there's nothing on your list that you're excited about, you might still set dates that you'll work toward. This will help you stay focused and working toward these things, even if they're small. The overall goal, of course, is to be at home with your children, but it's also helpful to set reachable, tangible goals as well.

It may seem overwhelming if your list is long. Just remember that if this is where God wants you and what He wants you to be doing, He'll give you everything you need. As work-at-home moms, we may have to live without the leather chair and the five-line phone, but we're blessed in many other—eternal—ways.

You'll also need items such as business cards and promotional materials. Vistaprint is one the premier places on the Web to have business cards printed. They also offer a full line of personalized products such as flyers, postcards, magnets, mailing labels, note cards, t-shirts, car magnets, and more. We subscribe to their mailing list, so we're notified of specials. They offer free business cards, but we upgrade so that there's not a Vistaprint ad on the back of the card to diminish the professionalism of our cards.

A great way to make your business cards memorable is to include your picture and/or business logo in the design. At most online business card web sites, you can upload a photo, logo, or even the entire design if you would like. If you watch for specials, you can get these upgrades at a great price. You'll look and feel like the professional you are.

Setting Up Your Desk

Regardless of the type of home-based business you choose, you'll need a desk to help you organize and manage business matters.

When I (Jill) first started working from home doing data entry, I thought I needed a big setup—separate office, desk, computer, and all the extras to make it feel like a *real* office. As my business developed and I began to focus on running CWAHM full-time, I began to realize that there were a lot of things—such as the office itself—that I didn't necessarily need.

Close to the time that our second child was to be born, we moved my desk and computer down into our family room in the basement. My former office became the new baby's nursery, and I had to get used to working in the open space of the family room with the distractions of toys and TV. Once I got used to it, I came to enjoy having my office in the family room. I'm able to work on and off throughout the day—even with the kids playing right in the same room.

Because my business is solely online, I've added a second computer; both computers have flat-panel monitors, allowing me to work on both computers at the same time. I keep my e-mail open on one computer and do web site work or writing on the other. This way I don't have to flip back and forth between programs when an e-mail comes in.

Having two computers set up this way also provides a backup. If one computer goes down, I have the other already set up and in use, so there's no downtime.

Organizing Your Home Office

It can be challenging for a work-at-home parent to maintain an organized home office. The office or desktop is often the last of your worries as you strive to raise children, support your spouse, and run a home-based business. However, keeping up with the clutter and chaos of your office may be just what you need to get you in a working mind-set and help you be more efficient when working.

Here are a few simple things you can do on a regular basis to help take some of the stress out of the organizing process:

- Address your home office/desktop chaos in blocks of time. You may want to set aside just a couple of hours, or you may need an entire day. Decide what works for you, and stick to it. If it's not possible for you to set aside a block of time to devote to organizing, consider using a headset so you can de-clutter while you take calls.

- Have the necessities on hand: trash can, pens, file folders, mail baskets, and other organization items that will enable you to sort, throw out, and find a place for each item. Envision your goal, and purchase the supplies necessary to create that environment.

- Clear the space you want to organize. Then make a pile of all the paper. Examine each paper and sort according to importance. Throw out as much as possible, and find a place for each of the other items.

- If you start feeling stressed, take a short break. Set a goal of how much you want to accomplish during the time you have available, and set an incentive for reaching the goal. It's always easier to complete a task when you know you'll be rewarded.

Once you've organized your office, it's important to take small steps every day to keep the room clean and tidy. It's very easy to fall back into the routine of piling things on your desktop and around the room. Here are ten simple tasks that you can do daily to help maintain your organized space:

1. Clean out your inbox. This can apply to snail-mail or e-mail. Create a special basket for postal mail that needs to be taken care of right away and another basket for items that can wait a day or two.

2. To keep your e-mail inbox under control, create folders within your e-mail program. Keep what needs to be done immediately in your inbox, and distribute the rest into your folders. You can also use "rules" in programs such as Outlook to help separate e-mail and make it easier to manage.

3. Make sure all notes are transferred to your calendar, hand-held computer, or day planner. It's very easy to pile up a desktop full of paper by writing every note on a Post-it. You can also create an "idea book" to catalog all your business ideas for future reference.

4. Remove all mail, catalogs, and magazines from your desk. Put them in their proper places as you receive them. This will considerably cut down the amount of clutter on your desktop.

5. File as you go. This is the most basic and most important tip of all. If you file as you go, your records will be in order, your desktop will be clear, and you will feel more professional.

6. Clean off your desktop each evening. There's nothing better than sitting down at a clean workspace each morning. It helps to keep your mind focused on your

business and makes finding important documents a snap.

7. Take the time to organize your desk. Put things away the first time in the appropriate section.

8. Go through your inbox and prioritize.

9. As you print something, file it, but first consider whether or not you really need a printed copy. If it's in your computer and backed up, do you need a hard copy?

10. Open mail and file immediately. Avoid piles at all costs.

By following these easy guidelines, you'll have a clean and organized home office in no time.

Whatever you do, work at it with all your heart, as working for the Lord, not for men *(Colossians 3:23).*

Telephone Basics

Phone jealousy! Every child we know suffers from it. It never fails—when you're on the phone, the kids will throw a tantrum, scream at the top of their lungs, or find a way to demand your attention. Here are some tips for handling this widely experienced problem.

An answering machine is an absolute necessity. You can let the answering machine take the message when you're occupied.

In order to keep interruptions to a minimum, consider adding a second phone line in your home for business calls. You have several options: you can either attach an answering machine to the business line or purchase voice mail to help manage your business calls. When necessary, you can turn off the ringer on the business phone so that a phone call will not bother you during family time or your children's naptime. A portable phone or cell phone is also convenient for times when you need to escape the noise.

Other Phone Considerations

Some businesses can benefit from an 800 number. Your clients can contact you toll-free, and it gives a professional appearance. Many companies offer inexpensive 800 numbers, and most can be forwarded to ring through to your home phone or business line. Jill uses PowerNetGlobal Communications (<www.pngcom.com>). Through this inexpensive service, phone calls can be forwarded through your 800 number to your home phone or whatever other number you choose. You can even request vanity 800 numbers, in which some or all of the numbers spell out a word.

Jill has also used a free online voice-mail service by Google called Google Voice (www.google.com/voice). It gives you a private number you can give out that rings straight to voice mail. Jill has it set up so that her toll-free number is forwarded to this private number, which is then answered by voice-mail. This provides a professional greeting that answers when a client calls, and the client is able to leave a message. This also allows Jill the freedom of calling back at a time that works best for her.

Depending on your business, you may feel it would be helpful to set up conference calls. Several programs are available. One of the most popularly used programs is Skype (<www.skype.com>). Not only can you make free computer-to-computer calls, but you can also pay a small fee to use Skype somewhat as a second phone line. You can make outgoing calls, receive incoming calls, and even make conference calls.

Skype has even added a video call feature that allows you to make video calls to other Skype users. All you need is a webcam. Many times when Jill's husband is traveling for work, they use Skype's video call feature. Jill and the kids sit in front of her laptop and can see Allen and chat with him while he's hundreds of miles away.

Web Site

Creating an online presence for your business is necessary, and you'll need a great web site. It may sound overwhelming if you're uncertain about how to begin to learn the basics of creating your first web site. It's actually much simpler than you might think. Listed below are a few tips and tricks to make your first web site pain-free.

First, you'll need a domain name. A domain name is what your web site visitors will type in to visit your site. For example, the domain name you would type in to find Christian Work at Home Moms is <www.cwahm.com>. Diana's is <www.virtualwordpublishing.com>, so "virtualwordpublishing" is the domain name portion of the web site address.

You can purchase a domain name at a reasonable rate at places across the Internet. On the main page of these sites you'll find a spot where you can search to see if the domain name you would like to purchase is available. The domain name you choose should be descriptive and easy to remember.

One way you can choose your domain name is to match your business name. Another great idea is to combine keywords that describe your business. In his book *Internet Riches: The Simple Money-Making Secrets of Online Millionaires,* Scott Fox recommends making a list of nouns and adjectives that describe your business and then combining them into a domain name. Examples he provided included <myitalianloafers.com> and <qualityshoes.com>.

Following are some tips on your domains:

- See that your domain registry accounts are up to date.
- Have a valid e-mail addresses listed to receive expiration notices when your domains need to be renewed.
- Keep access and information about the domain registry.
- Make sure you own the domain. If you have someone else set up the domain for you—which is often the case when you hire a web designer—you need to see that he or she has it registered in your name. You may also want to make sure you have a written agreement that the domain is under your ownership.

Your Internet connection is crucial for a successful business. Being able to connect and work online for submitting articles, press releases, even contacting clients is crucial to your success. Therefore, you want to choose a reliable host. This is extremely important, because it can affect not only your web site but your e-mail account as well.

It's important to read through the features of the hosting package you choose. Jill once had a web host that did not allow the hosting of MP3 files. MP3s are audio files and are necessary for podcasting, therefore an integral part of what she needed in a hosting account. Jill had to switch hosts because of this one crucial detail—costing her a lot of time and money that could have been avoided had she checked into the hosting account more thoroughly before signing up.

Take the time to go back over your web site and carefully read it. People are often in such a hurry to get a web site developed that they make typos and grammatical errors. When a new client comes to your site and sees typos and misspellings, he or she may lose confidence in your services.

Also, when you go to your site, do you like it? Do you see ways to improve it? Keep in mind that your site is a reflection of your business, so it pays to make it the best it can be.

Design and layout of your web site are very important. Make sure that your layout is clear and easy to navigate. If possible, include an easy-to-find and easy-to-navigate menu that contains all the different sections you've included on the site.

Take the time to make a list of everything you want your web site to include, complete with all the products, details, prices, and options your customers will want to know. Remember—the more information you give the customers up front without their having to search your web site, the more sales you'll make. Customers like clean, warm web sites that make them feel they have all the necessary information and can trust your business.

A few of the most important things to think about:

- How many pages will there be on your web site?
- What information is important? You should include at least a bio, services, prices, and testimonials, in addition to product descriptions.
- What features or products will you sell?
- Will a shopping cart be required?
- What colors do you want your web site to consist of?
- What benefits can you add that will attract your clients and keep them coming back?
- What keywords should be added to your site?
- Are you adding a blog or newsletter?
- How well do you know your demographic?
- What is the age of your target customer?
- What are the interests of your target customer? Hobbies? Goals?
- What will catch your potential client's eye?
- Will your web site be geared primarily toward women or men?
- What contact information do you want to use on your site?

Compile this information, and start mapping out the graphics, pictures, and text that you want to use on your site. Remember: visitors to your web site will want to scan your site easily for the information they need in order to make their purchase.

Use bulleted lists when possible, and keep your paragraphs to a maximum of a few sentences each.

Finally, you're ready to put your plans into action. If you feel you don't have the experience necessary to build a web site, we highly recommend hiring someone. Find a web designer with exceptional skills and commitment to the client's best interest.

You might want to consider a web site template. You can find excellent templates by doing an Internet search using the keywords *templates web design*. Find the template that meets all your needs. The template will give you a framework and allow you to somewhat fill in the blanks with the text and graphics you've chosen.

Hiring a Web Site Designer

A good web site designer can make a substantial difference in your business by helping you look better. It's important to have one you can trust. Choose a web designer you can count on to maintain your site and make good backups of your files. You don't want to lose your entire site if it crashes. Also, it's important to have a designer who will complete your work promptly. Discuss the turnaround time, and clearly state your expectations prior to hiring a web site designer. Get your agreement in writing.

A lot is involved in designing a web site. A designer should help you with layout, colors, and the flow of the site. You want your business site to be clean, efficient, and easy to use. Working with a good web site designer is a great way to achieve these goals.

When considering a designer, ask about the maintenance policies, and find one who is compatible with your needs. Cheaper is not always better. You could save a few dollars in the beginning, but if you have a designer who doesn't follow through, your site won't get the attention it deserves.

You'll need to decide if you want to hire a web designer who will build your web site from the ground up and do all maintenance. Depending on your budget, you may rather go with having a template created and then maintain it and make necessary modifications yourself. Diana and Jill are on opposite sides of the spectrum in this debate. Diana hires out all of her web work, while Jill does all her own design, hiring out only for programming.

No matter what type of web site design work you decide to go with, remember that the final product should be something that will be easy for your customers to use.

As mentioned earlier, it's critical to own your own domain and to make sure that the work your web site designer does belongs to you. This, too, should be addressed in the written contract between you and your designer. You're paying the designer to do work for you and design the site, but the site itself is your property. Many home business owners have learned this the hard way. They pay the designer without realizing that the designer retains copyright to the site. We believe that you should own your web site and all its contents. We encourage you to read the contract carefully and understand all the important details.

Also, keep all of the passwords and information you'll need to log into your hosting account. That way, if you and your web site designer part ways, you'll have access to your vital information. Diana has seen this happen in the past. A web designer had to give up her business due to personal reasons and unfortunately stopped working abruptly. Numerous web sites were affected.

Nancy Brown, a web site designer with <www.virtual galfriday.com> summarizes it nicely for us by stating, "If your web designer sets up the hosting and registers the domain, make sure you have all pertinent information in case of emergency, including URL of registrar; username/password for domain account and the URL of hosting account (how to log into your hosting account); username/password for your hosting account and when everything expires. Also, put the domain in your name, not the web designer's name."

There are some fabulous web site designers out there. Look at the portfolio of the designers you are considering. Does the designer's work match your personality? Does it look professional? Is it the same design over and over with little originality? When you consider these things, you can easily find the web site designer that's perfect for you.

Web Site Lingo

Here are a few basics terms:

Home page: This is the entrance to your web site—the visitor's first impression. This page will either keep people reading or it will cause them to move on to the next site. The front page is the key to your success. Make sure it's enticing. Also, get those keywords in there. *Note:* The *home* page is also commonly known as the *index* page.

Meta tags: These tags are embedded in your HTML and include the title of your page, its description, and keywords. You should provide a good description of the page using your best keywords. Make sure your tags are descriptive to the specific page, because this is the description that all search engines will display.

Site map: A site map is a page or section of the web site that contains a full layout of every page and topic on the web site. Many small web sites overlook this important feature, but it's a very simple way to give your visitors an overview of all you offer. Almost all large web sites use site maps to aid their customers.

HTML: Hypertext markup language. This is the programming language your web site is written in behind the scenes. Every color, image, link, and so forth has a specific tag in HTML.

WYSIWYG: What You See Is What You Get. WYSIWYGs are graphic interfaces for creating web sites. These programs allow you to create a web site without actually coding in HTML. Some examples are FrontPage and Dreamweaver.

URL: Uniform resource locator. This is another term for the web site address of a specific page on your web site. Every page of your web site has its own URL.

For example—

<http://www.cwahm.com> is the URL for the index page of CWAHM.

<http://cwahm.com/wordpress/about-us/belief-state ment/> is the URL for the CWAHM statement of faith.

<http://cwahm.com/wordpress/blog/> is the URL for Jill's blog.

Backlinks: These are links back to your site from other web sites. These help tremendously with your search engine rankings. We've gotten some of our best backlinks by writing articles and having our web sites listed in the "About the Author" or bio section of the articles.

Another great way to gain backlinks it to ask your clients to put your link on their web sites. Diana does publicity for clients, and by adding her name and site to their web sites, it creates a backlink for Diana's web site. This also benefits her clients by having the publicist listed there.

On CWAHM, Jill has HTML linking code available for anyone who would like to add a CWAHM backlink to his or her web site. In exchange for that link, Jill adds the person to the link directory on CWAHM.

Here's an example of the CWAHM text link code:

TEXT LINK:

Christian Work at Home Moms—CWAHM.com provides information and resources for home-based work and telecommuting jobs. CWAHM is dedicated to providing work-at-home moms opportunities to promote their businesses while at the same time providing them spiritual encouragement.

<http://www.cwahm.com>

URL: <http://www.cwahm.com>

HTML: <a href="http://www.cwahm.com">Christian Work at Home Moms</a>. CWAHM.com provides information and resources for home-based work and telecommuting jobs. CWAHM is dedicated to providing work-at-home moms opportunities to promote their businesses while at the same time providing them spiritual encouragement.

Keywords: These are words that search engines use to find and display web sites that match the terms someone is searching for. Keywords relate to the web sites being searched. Search engines pick up these words when they spider your site. You want keywords on your site that pertain directly to what you offer on your site.

Keyword rich: The content of your site has to be keyword rich. This means that the text on your web site is interspersed with keywords that the search engines will pick up. These keywords will help designate your web site in the search engine when someone searches for them. Also, keep the keywords to the top of the site. The closer your keywords are to the top of your site, the better chance they'll be picked up by search engines.

Spider: Search engines use programs called *spiders* to browse web sites and add them to the database. Spiders also visit most web sites on a regular basis to find changes and update the listing in their database.

Search engine: A search engine is an online program that Internet users can visit to search for a specific term or web site. Users can enter a keyword or phrase, and the search engine will return a listing of web sites that match.

SEO (Search Engine Optimization): SEO is the term used to describe the different methods one can use to help a web site place higher in search engine results. SEO can include keyword-rich meta-tags, content, and so forth.

Web Site Page Ranking

One important consideration for your web site is your Google page rank. This is a number between one and ten. It gives an idea of how popular your site is as calculated by Google's page rank algorithm. Take the time to download the

Google tool bar, and keep working to improve your ranking. A site with a rating of four or above is good. For complete definitions and instructions, visit <www.google.com/technology/>.

One of the first things Diana does for her publicity for clients is go to their sites through her web browser with the Google tool bar installed to see how well their sites are ranked. If the ranking is 0, she can advise them that they need to do more to get their keywords working. Also, if they have high page ranks, she can mention this to them, and it adds to their confidence in her public relations services.

There are several classes you can take to learn SEO, such as the free Yahoo Groups course, SEO Techniques, offered by J. Bailey of GNC Web Creations. You can pay someone to do it for you. It's well worth the investment. You can find an SEO professional by doing a Google search for "search engine optimization." Be sure you ask about qualifications and ask for recommendations.

Another way to see how your site compares to others is to use Alexa.com. Alexa shows traffic rankings that you can use to compare with other sites across the Web. You can view your traffic ranking, reach-per-million users, and page views per use. This can be a very handy tool to help you determine the popularity and reach of your web site. Take time to go there now to see how your page ranks. How did you do? If you're working on SEO, go back in a few months and see how far up your ranking has gone.

You can also check out other web sites to see how they compare. For example, at the time of the writing of this book, CWAHM.com has an Alexa traffic rank of 111,000. Diana's main web site, VirtualWordPublishing, ranks at 750,000. Not too bad for two crazy work-at-home moms.

Hopefully, this gives you a basic understanding of what it takes to have a highly rated web site. You've chosen a meaningful domain name, researched the demographic that you're trying to reach, and thought out the layout and other aspects of your web site in order to create a meaningful site that will be easy for your visitors to use. You're now ready to direct traffic to your web site and make sales.

5 MARKETING YOUR BUSINESS

Now that you've found the perfect business with the perfect products or services, it's time to think about marketing it. You'll discover that just as important as finding the right business is finding a way to market it so that others know it's available. Let's talk about how to approach that.

We provide some basic marketing tips here, but it's important to connect with others who successfully market your type of business. What are they doing that's making them successful? Find a mentor if you can, or pay for coaching. It's well worth it when you can get those marketing tips straight from someone who has already achieved a measure of success.

Keep in mind that marketing your Christian work-at-home business will depend a great deal on what type of business you operate. For example, Jill markets her web site differently than Diana markets her publicity business.

Jill relies heavily on word of mouth and search engine traffic. Because CWAHM serves a unique niche, the Christian work-at-home mom, her search engine rankings are high, and much of her web site traffic finds CWAHM that way. Jill also writes articles and contributes to books to help spread the word about her business. A few times each year, she takes out an ad either on a web site that captures her target market or a newspaper or magazine that does that. One feature of CWAHM is that most of the resources are free. That helps her tell others about her site and invite them to visit without pressure.

Diana markets mainly with press releases and articles, networking actively online, taking advantage of social networking, guest speaking, and getting word-of-mouth referrals.

To help you jumpstart your marketing, read the following interview with Maria T. Bailey, author of *Trillion Dollar Moms*. Maria is founder and CEO of BlueSuitMom.com. As the mother of four and former Fortune 100 executive, Maria watched information-starved mothers search for tools to help them balance their family responsibilities while maintaining a career. She's also the host of "Mom Talk Radio," a nationally syndicated radio show for moms, and host of "The Balancing Act" on Lifetime TV. She is also the creator of Smart Mom Solutions, a product line that offers solutions to everyday challenges for busy moms.

Jill: I'm curious—how did you get started doing what you do?

Maria: I had three children in less than twenty months. I actually was a marketing executive in a Fortune 100 company. I guess my two worlds collided because I was doing a lot in marketing to mothers, and I was traveling a lot and realized that there wasn't a place for working mothers to go to get information to help them balance work and family life; so I launched my first company, which was BlueSuitmom.com, and it just grew from there.

Jill: Do you think the marketing dynamic changes when it's moms marketing to other moms?

Maria: I think that when moms are marketing to other moms, they have better insights than a lot of companies. For instance, if you're a mom and you're running a business geared toward other moms, you probably have the insight to know that moms are answering their e-mail at night after their kids go to bed or during naptime. A company that's not as in touch with the everyday behaviors of moms doesn't have that insight. I think moms who are marketing to moms have better intuition, and they're working from a more knowledgeable starting place than a company that's not. This is especially true for companies run by men—you have to explain to them things like reasons you don't call a mom during nap time.

Someone who's running a home-based business should never think they won't be able to compete with the big guys. That's so untrue. If you think about it, you are actually living your target market, whereas Proctor & Gamble or Johnson & Johnson are not as nimble or as immersed in the market. They have to pay thousands and thousands of dollars to get the knowledge you have. You have to view working from a vantage point.

Jill: What are your top three tips when you try to give someone an insight into reaching moms?

Maria: Number one, I always say you have to walk in their shoes; you have to know how they're using your product. Why are they using your product? What problem or challenges are they trying to solve? What solutions does your product offer them? This is important, because a lot of times moms use products in ways that you, as the creator, never intended them to be used. We fall in love with our products; we fall in love with our company.

I'll give you an example. A few years ago I went to a company that makes plastic containers, and as a mom, I know that we use plastic containers for storing crayons, scrap booking materials, sewing kit supplies, and Legos—a whole bunch of things. I went into this conference room packed with men, and they told me the rubber containers were only for leftovers, that women use them to send leftover lunch with their husbands the next day. Well, clearly they don't know how consumers are using their products.

We did some research many years ago where we found that moms were using paper towels in almost 280 different ways, not just for getting spit-up off the floor. You really have to walk in the shoes of the consumer.

Number two, you need to be where moms are during the day. For example, sixty-five percent of all moms don't know what they're cooking for dinner at four o'clock in the afternoon. If you have a food product solution or meal solution, then what you want is to be on the radio in their cars to give them the solution of your product for dinner, because that's where moms are at four o'clock in the afternoon. You must walk in their shoes and present the solution to them when they need it and be where they are.

Think not only of the features of your product but also of what the benefit is to the mom. For example, if you live in a Southern state, many moms freeze their juice boxes to put into their kid's lunch box to keep the sandwich from getting soggy, and everything stays cold. The straw falls off one particular type of juice box if the product is frozen. If you truly know how a mom is using the product, then you'll know that the straw must stay on the box whether it's frozen or heated. So think about the benefit of the product. If you're the other guy whose straw does stay adhered, you should not only be talking about the 100-percent juice and the vitamin C but also the fact that the straw stays attached if you freeze the product. That's an added benefit to the mom. Think about the benefits and not just the features.

Jill: It's amazing that being aware of small details can have such a big impact on one's business. I think that's what I learned from *Marketing to Moms,* just thinking differently about business.

Maria: Jill, I know you haven't asked me this question, but you're talking about thinking differently, and I'd like to just make a comment on this in general about starting a business, because I feel very passionate about it.

In my career I've been fortunate to work with the entrepreneur of the world—he was named entrepreneur of the world—and three different billionaires who started companies—all men. The lesson I learned from these men about building companies is something a lot of moms who are starting home-based business take for granted.

We start these businesses because we love the idea of being home with our children, having flexibility, doing something we love, doing something that fulfills us, and we forget that we're building a business. We start our business with no business plan. We start it with no exit strategy. Every business should have an exit strategy. We start businesses without a clear vision of how we're going to make money at it. The main reason for that is because our motivation for starting a home-based business in the first place is not to make money. It's to facilitate a lifestyle that we want. Unfortunately, you must take a step back and say, "Am I spending most of my time trying to keep this business alive?" It takes the same amount of effort to run a business that makes money as it does a business that doesn't make money. In fact, sometimes it takes less effort to make money.

I would encourage women, knowing what I now know about starting a business, that you really need some kind of business plan, even if it's written on a napkin. Know where you want the business to go and how you're going to exit the business eventually. Are you building a business that could be bought by someone? Is it something that could be acquired or passed along to a neighbor or a friend, or are you grooming someone to take it over because there will be a day when your children will grow up? You want to be putting your effort into something that will make a little bit of money.

Jill: Tell me a little bit more about BSM Media, your journey, and some of the campaigns you've handled.

Maria: BSM Media is a full-service marketing-to-moms firm. It's a media company. There are two sides to our business. One side is that we own media properties geared toward moms, such as BlueSuitmom.com, newbaby.com, "Mom Talk Radio," and that's it right now. BSM media is the marketing side of the company, and we handle marketing programs and strategy for companies such as Precious Moments, Hewlett Packard, Disney. We've worked with Warner Brothers, Cartoon Network. We've had the privilege of working with a lot of big companies, and we also work with a lot of entrepreneurs, really great entrepreneurs such as Lisa Druxman of Stroller Strides, Julie Clark of Baby Einstein Video, and Liz Lange of Liz Lange Maternity. We work on everything from research to strategy to product design—anything that has to do with moms.

Jill: Tell me about *Trillion Dollar Moms.*

Maria: *Trillion Dollar Moms* is my latest book. It focuses on the generational differences of mothers. This is the first time in history we've had three distinct generations of moms. It's geared toward the research of the different generations of moms.

That left me breathless. We encourage you to think about the things Maria said in relation to your own business.

Diana had the good fortune to be mentioned in Maria's first book, and she and Maria live in the same area. Diana has watched Maria's success grow and has also seen many others achieve success by following Maria's advice.

Listen to advice and accept instruction, and in the end you will be wise *(Proverbs 19:20).*

Press Releases

Press releases are an excellent way to gain publicity for your business. As Melody Spier of Essential Office Support states, "Using publicity and press releases to establish your credibility, build your reputation, and position yourself as an expert is one of the easiest ways to sell more products and services. The best thing about publicity is that it's free. By regularly writing and submitting quality articles and press releases, you will see a marked increase in the number of visitors to your site and in sales."

You can pay hundreds of dollars for advertising only to have it come to a halt the minute you quit paying, or you can write articles and press releases for newspapers, ezines, newsletters, magazines, web sites, and so forth, and keep your name visible forever—*for free!*

If you don't have time to write your own press release or you're unsure of where to submit it, hire someone to do it for you. Consider hiring a publicity virtual assistant.

One of the most important things to consider when writing a press release, or "news release," as it's commonly referred to, is to make it newsworthy. We encourage you to go to <www.prweb.com> for their press release requirements. This site will also provide you with some great tips on what works and what doesn't.

Remember that editors want to see things done correctly. Many good releases get tossed just because they aren't set up properly. Your release is going to get a ten-second glance from a busy editor, which will determine whether or not it's accepted. In that ten seconds, you must let the editor know that you've done enough research to warrant space in his or her newspaper, magazine, or web site.

When writing a release, remember that the mere fact that you've started your own business is not enough to warrant publication. *Many* home-based businesses are vying for that space. It's important not only to describe your business but also to define its benefits to others. Highlight benefits you provide that directly meet the wants and needs of your readers.

When possible, tie your press release to current events and what's happening in the media by keeping an eye on the news and thinking of ways to tie your products or services into that. For example, Diana wrote about how great it was to be at home with her children during flu season. During rising unemployment, she writes on starting a virtual assistant business as an option for those looking for work.

Press releases are not just for newspapers anymore. Your target audience and potential clients are apt to read your releases online. This allows you a better opportunity to talk directly to your buyers or clients.

* * *

Following are pointers for writing a press release.

Write "FOR IMMEDIATE RELEASE" on the top left of the page.

Your contact name, phone number, e-mail address, and web site address follow. Some will include a physical address. We usually don't, but consider your audience and release in making that decision.

The headline is next, usually in bold and centered on the page. Summarize what the release is about to capture the reader's attention.

The body of the press release starts with the location of the release and the date.

For example:

Margate, Florida (May 2010)

Then comes the body of the release. Most press releases are 350-500 words, and we recommend no more than one page. The first paragraph contains the most important information. Don't save the best for last, because it won't be read. Editors need to be compelled to read your release. Include a unique angle, and you should also tie it in to the title. For some releases—such as those telling about an event—include the who, what, when, where, and how in this paragraph.

It's recommended that you write press releases in third person and use short sentences and paragraphs. However, we're seeing the third-person requirement changing. Check the latest guidelines for recent changes to formatting. Avoid using *I* and *me*. These terms are too personal for a business release.

Target your release. You'll be sending the release to a specific audience, so make sure it appeals to that audience. What information don't they know that you can supply? Nothing works better than to get an "aha" when the release is read.

Provide statistics. Do your research, and find relevant information that applies. You can easily do this through Google and other online means. Once you find your quote, do an online search on that particular topic. However, don't stop on the first link you come across and take that as expert advice. Research it a bit further, and make sure it comes from a well-known company or magazine, being careful of quotes from someone else's web site. Consider what makes him or her an expert. He or she may well be an expert on this topic, but make sure before you quote him or her. Also, it's important to quote correctly and get permission when necessary before you quote someone.

Include relevant quotes from experts in your field that will reinforce what you're saying. Approach authors, leaders in the industry, and other experts that back up the facts you're using. They'll normally appreciate the added publicity, and you get the quote you're looking for. For example, we're often asked to provide quotes for articles on home-based businesses. We welcome the opportunity, as it provides additional publicity for us.

If you have a satisfied client who you feel will add credibility to your release, you can add a quote from him or her.

Finally, since you're the expert, provide a quote from yourself. It's your opportunity to get to tell a little about the business from your perspective.

Be careful not to include so many outside sources that the release loses personal touches that make it uniquely yours. Additionally, the first time you mention an expert, give his or her full name, and then refer to him or her by last name only.

The last paragraph should be your call to action. You've talked about your business or products—now tell readers what to do with the knowledge they've just acquired. For example, make it clear where readers can go to purchase your products, find your web site, and so forth.

Indicate the end of the release with "###." You may also include a short "about the company" paragraph here.

When including your web site, include http:// in front of the www so that web browsers will recognize it and make it a "live" link. This means that readers will be able to click on the web address, and it will take them to your web site. It's also best for search engines to pick up.

When submitting press releases and articles online, you'll probably be asked to provide a summary and keywords. Take your time when you write these, and use your keywords effectively. Write the summary to compel someone to read your press release. Don't make it too promotional. You want to entice them to *want* to read your release.

When writing press releases and articles, it's important to save them as text (.txt) documents or copy them into a text file such as the "Notepad" program that comes standard on most computers before you submit them online. Copy and paste from text files rather than Microsoft Word, because Word has a tendency to change the characters of the text—then, when you paste this into the site where you're submitting your release, you end up with strange characters in your release. For example, Word will often replace bullets with illegible characters.

You can easily save your documents as .txt files from within Word by going to "File," then "Save as," and then choosing "Plain Text" from the drop-down menu. Of course, always double-check when in the review portion of submitting your release that it all looks fine.

Press releases really do work. Diana recently had a release accepted by PRWeb, and it then went on to hit several major newspapers and media outlets. Through a Google alert for her city of Margate, Florida, a local journalist saw it and contacted her. Also, one of her clients had a press release accepted at one of the free submission sites, and *USAToday* picked up the story.

Visit CWAHM.com for a brief listing of places to submit press releases. Be advised that these constantly change. To find free submissions, do an Internet search for "submitting press releases," or hire a virtual assistant to assist you.

Here are some places we recommend for submitting your releases:

Free Releases—although you can pay to get better results

\<www.openpr.com\>

\<www.bignews.biz\>

\<www.ideamarketers.com\>

\<www.pressmethod.com\>

\<www.pr-usa.net\>

\<www.sanepr.com\>

\<www.przoom.com\>

\<www.powerhomebiz.com\>

\<www.newswiretoday.com\>

\<www.pr-canada.net\>

\<www.prurgent.com\>

\<www.pressreleasepoint.com\>

\<www.free-press-release-center.info\>

Paid Submission Sites

\<www.prweb.com\>

\<www.sbwire.com\>

\<www.webwire.com\>

\<www.prnewswire.com\>

\<www.businesswire.com\>

\<www.1888pressrelease.com\>

\<www.pr9.net\>

\<www.pressreleasenetwork.com\>

\<www.usanews.com\>

\<www.free-press-release.com\>

\<www.pressbox.co.uk\>

\<www.ereleases.com\>

\<www.eworldwire.com\>

\<www.blackpr.com\>

<www.prleap.com>

<www.expertclick.com>

Resource Directories—to find where to submit

<www.newslink.org>

<www.rtir.com>

When submitting press releases, especially when using the larger services such as PRNewswire, make sure you know all costs involved, including those for submitting a photo. Many press submission sites add a photo at no cost. However, the larger ones charge for this feature. In fact, Diana recently discovered that a small graphic of a book cover cost $400 in addition to the cost of running the release. It was a costly mistake, but a valuable lesson.

We recommend signing up for Joan Stewart's Publicity Hound course on writing a press release (<www.publicity hound.com>). It's free. Also, sign up for Bill Stoller's Free Publicity Newsletter (<www.publicityinsider.com>) for excellent information on public relations as well as media connections. Visit Susan Harrow's site, www.prsecrets.com, for amazing information on getting publicity. To receive media leads from reporters, check out <www.helpareporter.com>, which is free; Profnet from PRNewswire at <www.prnewswire.com>, which charges; and <www.prleads.com>, which also charges.

Let love and faithfulness never leave you; bind them around your neck, write them on the tablet of your heart (*Proverbs 3:3*).

Writing and Submitting Articles

Article writing is another effective way to market your business. It establishes you as an expert and gets more online exposure when you utilize your carefully selected keywords. We suggest you try to make article writing a regular part of your marketing strategy.

There are significant differences in where you distribute press releases and where you submit articles. Press releases are generally sent to newspapers and television and radio stations. Articles are usually sent to web sites and blogs. Another difference is that in press releases you're allowed to put your hyperlinks and web site address in the release itself. With articles, that information is included in the bio.

Articles allow you to write on topics you know, and it's easier to provide how-to information. It's important, too, that you actually *do* know what you're writing about. That may seem obvious to you, but we've seen a lot of people try to write articles on topics they aren't familiar with, because they believe that's what their target audience wants. Your goal in writing articles is to make the reader say, "Wow—she knows her stuff!"

Write to your target audience. What do they want to hear? What benefits and information can you provide that they might not already know? You can be specialized in a certain area; however, there are a lot of people out there who don't have the knowledge you do. Writing about it truly helps.

Remember your keywords, and put the most powerful keywords in the title and in the first few paragraphs.

It's important when writing articles to keep the length of each section within the length requirements requested by the entity you're submitting to. If your article is too long or too short, it won't post. You also won't be informed that it isn't posting—it just won't be accepted.

Following are some guidelines to follow if your article needs to be shortened before you submit it.

Titles: 125-150 characters—*cannot* be ALL CAPS

Summary: 400-500 characters

Bio: 1,000 characters—or four to six lines

Keywords: 100-200 characters

Article length: 500-1000 words

Articles are best when they stick to one subject or theme. Don't try to share too much information. Get the reader's attention with a "hook"; then give a "call to action" to spur the reader into what you want him or her to do—visit your web site, buy your book, buy your product, etc.

Don't make your article sound like a sales pitch. A lot of places might accept it, but the reader is going to get bored. When you provide the audience with information they need, then they'll look at your bio to see who wrote it.

And speaking of bios, include a good one. This should be information on how the reader can find out more about you and your company. Your bio should include your contact information, the title of any books you've authored, and your web site information. We also include a line that states the article is free to reprint as long as the author's bio remains intact. If you have something to give away, mention it to help draw readers to your web site. It's important to take them directly to the page on the site where this exists, that is, the landing page.

We recommend creating several bios and fine-tuning them. Keep in mind that you need to spark enough interest in your bio to catch the reader's eye. Make it enjoyable and not just fact after fact.

Your work is not done when you've completed writing the article. You must spend time double-checking your article for accuracy. If it goes out with typos or the wrong web address, the time spent writing it has been wasted.

Post your articles where they'll have the most impact. Don't waste your time posting a business article on a crafting web site, for example. One of the reasons we feel that our article submissions have been so successful is that we research where to put those articles that will pack the most punch. Research takes time, but you can start a list and eventually have quite a database per topic. We've created a database in Excel so that when we want to send it out, it's easy to do.

Do an Internet search on your topic and/or your name, and follow up to see if someone has accepted your article. Then send future articles to them. Once you know they're interested in your topic, you're ahead of the game.

Diana asks her clients to sign up for Google alerts under their names, business names, and topics. When one of their articles or press releases is posted and it gets picked up by Google, they can see it. We also set up a Google alert for the title of the article in quotes. That way you can see even further where the article goes, because it will bring those results in as well.

Diana also signs up for Google alerts under topics of interest such as *virtual assistant* and *working at home*. Then when a newspaper, web site, blog, or so forth writes on it, she follows up with her article or her client's article. If they wrote on it once, they likely will write on it again.

Many businesses today are signed up for Google alerts, which is a prime reason to submit articles often. When people are looking for that topic, they'll click on it to read your article too. For instance, if readers are looking for topics on college courses, and you mention "college" in the headline, anyone who has googled that term will see your article.

Also, before you start, do a Google search on your own name. Then, every month run a Google search, and you'll see the results. Of course, hopefully the sales alone will tell you that the efforts are working, but this is a good indication too. One great thing with article and press release writing is that even months later that site could get spidered, and your article will get top recognition again.

If you have a script on your site, such as Google analysis, that will tell you where people are coming from. You can see where the articles are accepted and focus your efforts more there.

Here are some tips to consider when submitting articles:

- Don't put too many web site links in the article itself. Instead, use your bio to include links and get the exposure you want. However, be sure that your bio doesn't sound strictly like an advertisement.

- People love to see how-tos in an article. Provide them with information they don't already know. Then list it in bullets or numbered in the article. Readers especially like the top five tips or the top tips to something.

- Have a point. Don't write articles just to hear yourself type. Make sure that every article you write is some-

thing you can be proud to have authored and will genu-
inely enrich the reader.

- Syndicate your articles. Find web sites such as Idea
  Marketers.com that will allow you to submit multiple
  articles for syndication. If possible, purchase credits to
  gain more exposure for your article on their web sites.
  You'll be surprised at how many people will sign up to
  syndicate your articles on their web sites if your articles
  are well written.

What is syndication? It's a term used when articles that
you've written are posted on many different web sites or in
print. Web sites are available to help you syndicate your writings, such as Ideamarketers.com. You input your articles, and
they provide code for anyone who signs up to syndicate your
articles on their own web sites. Then, their web sites are automatically updated anytime you post a new article.

Visit our web site for a listing of places to submit articles
and article samples. You can find more by performing online
searches for terms such as "free places to submit articles," "article submissions," "free articles for reprint," "submit articles,"
and so on.

Here are a few of our favorite article submission web sites:

ISNARE.com: <http://www.isnare.com>
EzineArticles.com: <http://www.ezinearticles.com>
IdeaMarketers.com: <http://www.ideamarketers.com>
Digital-Women.com: <http://www.digital-women.com/submit
article.htm>

MomsEzine.com: <http://www.momsezine.com/articles.html>

GoArticles.com: <http://www.goarticles.com>

Buzzle.com: <http://buzzle.com>

Article Alley: <www.articlealley.com>

Article City: <www.articlecity.com>

ArticleTrader: <www.articletrader.com>

Article Sphere: <www.articlesphere.com>

Article Biz: <www.articlebiz.com>

Amazines: <www.amazines.com>

ArticleDashboard.com: <www.articledashboard.com>

WorkAtHomeSuccess.com: <http://workathomesuccess.com/Articles/articles.htm>

BusinessKnowHow.com: <http://www.businessknowhow.com>

WebProNews.com: <http://www.webpronews.com/submit.html>

Self Growth: <www.selfgrowth.com>

Promotion World: <www.promotionworld.com>

Ezine Writer: <www.ezine-writer.com.au>

Author Connection: <www.authorconnection.com>

Expert Articles: <www.expertarticles.com>

SearchGuild: <www.searchguild.com>

Message Boards

A message board is an online place for moms to get together to share ideas, vent frustrations, or just chat. One way to market your business is to become involved. You can become a member and post, moderate a forum, or run your own message board.

Another advantage of posting on active message boards is that often the media scans those boards to find people for articles. Another benefit is that clients who read positive posts about you on message boards may want to work with you. That's why it's always important to be professional and offer good advice if others ask. You then become an expert.

Newsletters

Newsletters are a great way to market your business. Sending out a monthly or weekly newsletter is a great reminder to your customers about your business. Newsletters get your name in front of your potential clients, regular clients, and peers while showing your expertise and professionalism. They're an excellent means to market and grow your business and also show your existing clients your creative abilities. Jill notes that her sales are highest on the days her newsletter is sent.

If you're going to send out a newsletter, though, it's imperative that your newsletter is worthy of being read. We both subscribe to a lot of newsletters, but there are only a few that we always read when they arrive. When Diana decided to create a newsletter, one of the first things she did was look at those newsletters she always reads and determine what it is about them that makes her want to read them. What sets them apart from the others?

One of the important features she discovered about those regularly read newsletters was that they provided her with valuable information to help her in her business and that the information they shared with her helped her make a greater profit—often information she didn't already know. For example, some newsletters provided tips on search engine optimization, public relations resources and tips, new affiliate programs, or software shortcuts. Since she's always eager to grow her business, information on those topics is valuable.

When writing your newsletter, think about what expert knowledge you have or can obtain that would interest your targeted market. That's what you want to add to your newsletter.

Keep the following points in mind:

Your Readers

- Know your readers and what they want.
- Ask your readers for feedback and ways to improve.
- Talk to your readers. Don't just give information; think about that audience out there reading your newsletter. How do they feel after reading what you've written?

Your Writing Style

- Use short, simple sentences, keeping paragraphs short.
- Write clearly, and avoid slang or profanity.
- Use humor, and keep a refreshing tone to your writing.
- In keeping your tone friendly, also keep it professional.
- Have white space between the paragraphs.
- Use small graphics whenever applicable.
- Include your logo for business recognition.
- Use plain text, 12- to 14-point font.
- Be consistent so your style is recognizable.

Headings

- Entice the reader with your heading to ensure that he or she reads the articles. Most people decide whether they'll even read the article from the heading.
- Headlines should be slightly larger than the other text.
- Use bold or italics, but don't use all caps.

- Make sure that the heading and article talk about the same topic. It's great to have an awesome heading, but if your article is on something else, you lose the edge you just gained.

Content of Newsletter

- Content is king. Just as on your web site, it's vital to have your newsletter or ezine packed full of useful information.

- Provide articles written by you and other experts.

- Provide any new services or features you've added to your business.

- Provide links of relevant press releases, articles, other sites, and so forth. This gives readers more information they can review.

- Provide case studies, facts not known, and so forth. Sign up for Google News so you can get information your clients might not have seen.

- Provide a collection of valuable small business tips, testimonials, and so forth.

- When providing tips, provide lists such as "The top ten reasons to . . ."

- Provide a personal message from you. Many readers enjoy hearing how you're doing and what's new in your life and business. Just don't go overboard.

- Provide humorous quotations or jokes.

- Contests * Polls * Freebies * Quizzes * Games * Let the fun begin. Why not include something that makes the reader look forward to taking a break from his or her busy day to read your newsletter?

- If you want to make money with your newsletter, put in ads or Google Adsense.

The Final Step: Proofing

- Make sure everything is 100-percent accurate, with no typos.
- Make sure you have permission for the use of any copyrighted material.
- Make sure you've credited any sources correctly.
- Make sure that what's about to go out reflects well on your business.

Most ezines are "opt-in," which means that all those who receive it have actually registered to receive it—they want it already. Your end of the bargain is to provide them great information that keeps them wanting it every time. Once you find a winning strategy, stick with it—no need to change every month. Let your readers get used to your style and way of writing.

Jill has used many newsletter programs over the years and finally settled with YMLP.com (Your Mailing List Provider) a few years ago. She searched high and low to find the best pricing and the most features. Her primary concerns were to have the ability to customize the message, to have an opt-in list that helps to combat spam, and the ability to schedule the newsletter to send out at a specific date and time.

Diana uses Constant Contact and loves it. It has templates that enable her to easily customize a newsletter, promotional piece, and so forth. She can also easily keep track of how many people opened it and whether or not they clicked on any links provided and what links they clicked on. It's opt in, so people who receive it have requested to be on her list. Plus, she uses it to send out press releases of her clients to her subscribers as well.

One caution: be careful when using free newsletter services. Many times they contain ads over which you have no control and may be contradictory to your beliefs. When Jill first started out, she used a free service. While this option worked, she had no control over the ads that the service included. After only a few months of using the free option, Jill knew she needed to have full control over what was contained in her newsletter and opted to begin paying for a newsletter service.

There are a couple of different formats for newsletters. You can write up an all-text newsletter or format your newsletter using HTML, which can be read by most e-mail programs.

Always check anti-spam laws to make sure you're including all the necessary information, such as unsubscribe instructions and a mailing address.

Building Mailing and E-mail Lists

A mailing list is an amazing tool for building your business. A mailing list is a collection of names, e-mail addresses, and other information gathered from people who would like to receive information from you. A mailing list can be used for newsletter mailings, e-mailing specials, and many other forms of communication between you and your clients.

Most Internet marketers will advise you that capturing those e-mail addresses and creating your mailing address are mandatory to promoting your business. As those lists grow, so does your opportunity to be in front of people who have showed interest in your products or services.

Jill set a goal one year to build her mailing list and break the 5,000-subscriber mark. She began researching the best ways to get web site visitors to subscribe, and by the end of that year she was well over 5,000.

During that year, Jill gained a lot of insight into making a newsletter visible and causing people to *want* to receive it. For example, she began offering freebies to new subscribers. Current subscribers often receive special updates of events and promotions that are available only to those on her subscriber list.

Jill also organized her newsletter into an easily readable format and began adding in consistent weekly topics such as featured articles, recipes, and even a craft project for kids. Another weekly section features tips that subscribers send in sharing unique ways they build their businesses. This started out as a summer-only section, but she had such an overwhelmingly positive response that she's been able to keep this section running for more than two years. Each week she has women sending in tips. This is a win-win situation. The newsletter gets great content, and the women get their business name and web site included and sent out to all the subscribers.

> Many, O LORD my God, are the wonders you have done. The things you planned for us no one can recount to you; were I to speak and tell of them, they would be too many to declare *(Psalm 40:5)*.

Speaking Engagements

Once you've established yourself in business, you may be asked to speak or give teleseminars on topics related to your business. These opportunities may be online events, such as home-based business expos or podcasts, teleseminars, or they may be held locally at places like the Chamber of Commerce or a local moms' group. This can be a way to generate sales for your business and establish yourself as an expert in your field.

It's important to be prepared. Here are some tips for preparing:

- Know your audience and where they are in their businesses. If you prepare a segment and the information you provide is over your audience's heads, it can have a negative effect. They want information they can relate to. You won't be able to please everyone, but by taking the time to know your audience better, you'll have a much better chance of providing the information most of them are seeking.

- Be prepared. Naturally, you want to prepare yourself on the information you'll be talking about, but also prepare yourself for questions. Think about the topic and what could be asked. This helps you be ahead of the game when it comes to question-and-answer time.

- We usually prefer to save questions until the end, and if that's acceptable to the host, that works out well. Or talk on a topic, break for questions, and then move on to a new topic. What generally happens when you allow questions throughout your discussion is that you get sidetracked and find it hard to get back on track. Once in a while you'll come across someone who wants individualized mentoring. They'll ask questions specific to their business, and if you answer those specific questions, you won't have time to share the information you want to give the general audience. When this happens, politely say, "I can see you have a lot of questions, and I'd love to address them all, but I'm afraid that our time is limited here. Could you e-mail me those later?" We've found that if you say, "I'll answer all those questions at the end," that one person can take up all the question-and-answer time. We've also encountered people who keep asking questions long after the event ends. A little mentoring time is fine, because after all, you do want to help. However, you must not let a one-hour teleseminar take up an entire afternoon.

- Try to get e-mail addresses or invite listeners to your site, and ask them to sign up for your newsletter. You want to promote your book, your site, whatever you're offering. Inviting them to your web site is a subtle way of saying, "Check it out and see if you're interested."

- Give away something. This gives the attendees something to remember you by and a reason to e-mail you.

Networking

Developing business relationships and friendships is a great way to grow your business, and the benefits of networking will have a positive impact on your business. You'll receive confidence through the reinforcements that you're doing the right thing. You'll develop connections with others in your given field. It also combats the isolation some women experience when working from home.

One way you can network is to become a part of a local moms' group and fellowship with others in your same situation. There are many moms who are feeling the same things you are. Find them. In helping them, you just may help yourself.

Networking can help you grow spiritually and professionally. Once you begin spending time with other professionals in your field, you'll find a few select people who will motivate and push you to do more than you ever thought you could.

Remember to give back to the people who are part of your network. Don't just ask questions and never give feedback; it's important for you to contribute too. What you give out will usually come back to you tenfold.

Develop your thirty-second description of your business and what you do. Sometime this is called an elevator speech, because it should be short enough but descriptive enough that you can explain your business to another person in the time it takes to ride the elevator a couple of floors. What it is about your business that person would want to know? Perfect it so it comes naturally when you're asked so you can deliver it in under a minute.

Continually search for new places to meet people and network. Running a home-based business is hard work, and you can never stop working at it if you want to be successful.

We also encourage you to find a mentor—if possible, someone who's in the same line of work as you are. She can help ease your transition into working at home, and you can learn from her successes and failures.

It's important that this person is someone you're comfortable with who will answer your questions and share her ups and downs with you. Also, be aware of how much you ask of your mentor. Most mentors truly want to help. But don't expect her to do the legwork and set up your business for you.

Networking allows you to let your potential clients know who you are and that you have a business. It can be an integral part of your business and a wonderful tool to get clients. Diana has often said that she can turn a simple "Hi—how are you?" into a marketing lead. She loves what she does, and she loves telling people about it. She does not pass up many opportunities to share.

Two are better than one, because they have a good return for their work *(Ecclesiastes 4:9).*

Networking Online

Networking and making business contacts can be some of the toughest aspects of running a home-based business, but they're also one of the most successful ways to develop your business. You must constantly find creative ways to meet new people and introduce them to your product. If you're working from home with small children around, this becomes even more difficult. Networking online may be the solution.

There are several ways to network online. An inexpensive way is to visit message boards. You can register on message boards for free and post any topic on the board that interests you. This is a good way to meet other Christians who also work from home and to develop Christian business relationships.

Another way to make business contacts online is through networking web sites such as LinkedIn, Facebook, and Twitter. We find these sites useful for building relationships with potential clients as well as establishing brand recognition. Networking with people through social web sites helps people realize that you're accessible, and that builds trust.

There are also networking groups on web sites such as Yahoo, Google and MSN. You can search for groups on these sites by topic and join for free. Countless Christian groups as well as work-at-home networks can be found on these sites. These groups generally are e-mail-based, so you'll receive e-mail from the group that will be formatted similarly to message board posts. This allows you the flexibility to read them when you have the time and choose the topics that interest you from the subject line. Many groups will allow you to place ads and generate conversation about your home-based business. Just check the guidelines before posting, and watch the group a couple of days before becoming active. You can then get a general feel for how that group works.

One very important and often overlooked way to make online contacts is to include your business name and web site address in the signature of every e-mail you send. This makes people aware of your business and allows them to easily visit your web site. Including your web site link—and maybe a catchy slogan also—will catch the reader's eye and give him or her easy access to your site.

If you send fifteen e-mails in a typical day, you'll have fifteen more individuals who know about your business. An e-mail signature is also a way to ensure that your current customers can effortlessly find your web site. It's important that customers find it with minimal searching, and an e-mail signature is one of the easiest ways to achieve this.

Networking online is a great way to meet people without having to leave your home. The Internet is one of the best resources available to home-based business owners. Once you have an idea of how and where to network online, you'll be well on your way to a successful new form of marketing.

Social Networking

There's no denying the power of social networking. It's easy, and the potential is great; you can definitely lose out on opportunities if you aren't active online. Simply put, social networking is building relationships—as you do in business networking—but in a more "social" setting. *Social networking* is a term that was originally used for any type of social gathering, but now it's best known as an online presence and the driving force on web sites such as Facebook, Twitter, MySpace, and others. It's in this social networking arena that businesses connect with their customers, and friends connect with each other on a personal, social level.

Twitter. Forget the "I don't care what they ate for lunch" attitude. Twitter is where your competition and peers are, and you need to be there too. Granted, there will always be a few who will update you every time they back out of their driveway, but that's rare. More and more businesses are networking and connecting with each other—and their customers—in ways never thought possible. It's more than just networking. Business owners can have chats, host events, get publicity for articles and press releases, and even announce seminars and radio shows.

To ensure success, it's important to learn the Twitter lingo. *Hashtags, Retweets, Fans,* and *Follow Friday* are just a few of many Twitter terms you need to know to do business better. It sounds overwhelming, but if you keep it simple and take it a step at a time, you can do it. When you come across a term you don't know, look it up right away; write down your interpretation, and investigate to find out more about it. The key is to constantly work to build your networks.

Facebook is more self-explanatory. The key here is to spend some time expanding your network. Fortunately, you will receive notices when someone responds to your posts—although you can turn these messages off if they get out of hand—so try to follow up as soon as you can. Be careful of your time management, though. Don't allow yourself to get sidetracked too often or for too long at a time.

We recommend that you make use of sites such as Twitter and Facebook to follow the experts in your industry and take advantage of their knowledge. It will feel almost as if you're walking around with them and looking over their shoulders and overhearing their success secrets. What's remarkable is how freely the experts give tips; we would be remiss not to take advantage of the information. It will help grow your business to listen to what's being said, to go to the sites that are recommended, and to actually do the things they suggest.

The upside to all this social networking is that relationships are built—and building relationships is the lifeblood of your business. Take time to connect with friends and fans on a personal level. It's no longer about posting your products and prices every day. It's about being real, being accessible, and truly connecting with your contacts.

Podcasts and Internet Radio

Allen Hart, Jill's husband and a computer systems administrator, defines podcasts and Internet radio best:

> To better understand podcasting, think of it as an online radio program delivered straight to your iPod or other MP3 player. Podcasts that have been created for just about every topic under the sun. A lot of podcasts focus on technology-related news and opinions, but the landscape of what's being done in podcasting is constantly evolving. I've found podcasts for everything from video games to Christian music. I would say that with podcasting, just like the Internet, the sky's the limit.

Many moms have asked us the difference between a podcast and an Internet radio show. The simplest definition we've come up with is that podcasts can be downloaded and listened to on any MP3 device, while Internet radio shows are generally listened to only online. Many Internet radio shows are also available as podcasts and are therefore available to be downloaded to your computer or MP3 device and listened to at your leisure.

Podcasting has many uses for the home-based business owner. It can be useful not only as a means of advertising but also as a way to communicate your business message. Plus, it's a great way to get free publicity by becoming a guest.

Podcasters are always looking for guests. E-mail them with topics you would like to discuss, and ask if their listeners would be interested. Here are some things that entice Jill when someone requests to be on her show:

- Unique topic: It's very helpful to approach hosts and explain your unique platform or topic that will stand out from the crowd and make listeners want to tune in.

- An engaging presence: Some people have a presence about them that makes them fun to listen to. If you have examples of other radio interviews you've done or speaking engagements you've been involved in, include those links when e-mailing radio hosts.

- An established following: If you have a following, a mailing list, a fan group, or another group of people you can contact about your interview, let the host know this. A host is more likely to choose a guest with a mailing list that can bring extra exposure to the show. Plus, the host is giving you a great opportunity by interviewing you. Do your part by making it as successful as possible.

- A web presence: It's very important in this day and age to have a web site that the host can direct listeners to.

- An available product or service: You should have a product or service you want to publicize. If you have a book or product launching in three months—wait. You want that audience to have an opportunity to purchase from you immediately.

Podcast Tips

Here are five ways podcasting can benefit your business:

It helps you reach your niche market. Depending on your product, podcasting can be the perfect way to reach new groups of people in your market. Believe it or not, there are people out there looking for the product you provide, and this enables them to find you.

Podcasts can be used as an advertising venue as well. A podcast that's listed in podcasting directories such as iTunes will reach thousands, even millions, of listeners. This can be a very inexpensive method for advertisers on a budget.

It helps you share your passion. Podcasting is a great way to share what you love. If you're excited about a topic or product, chances are there are others who are excited about it. A podcast connects you with others who share that same passion.

Note: People can hear your excitement over the airwaves. I always enjoy listening to a program that features a speaker who is obviously energized about his or her topic. When recording your podcast, keep a smile on your face, and allow your excitement to show.

It helps you communicate information. Successful home-based businesses flourish because they fill a need. A podcast can help this information reach the people it's intended to benefit. For example, CWAHM.com was created to help women be at home with their children while still contributing to their families financially. Many of the site's visitors are busy moms who may not have the time to scour the hundreds of pages the site contains. Research your topic and find all the interesting and little-known tips your listeners want to hear. Keep your listeners interested, and they'll want to hear more.

It helps establish you as an expert in your field. You must be willing to take the time, do the research, and share information that's valuable and useful to your listeners. Just as authors become experts by researching and writing on specific topics, podcasters become experts by sharing the information they uncovered with their listening audience.

It helps you reach your audience with little or no start-up costs or financial investment. In most cases, there's no need to be tech-savvy to be a podcast creator. It can be as simple as using a phone to record your podcast through a service such as Odeo.com or AudioAcrobat.com. There are, of course, more complicated setups. But to begin, you really need only a topic, a phone, and a quiet spot to record.

If you decide to begin a podcast, be sure to make it sound professional. Find an audio editing program, and do your best to remove any background sounds and "Ummmmms." Your podcast is an extension of your business, and you want your professional image to shine through.

Podcast and Radio Interview Dos and Don'ts

Going from working in your bathrobe to a public platform can be intimidating, but these tips will help lessen the stress.

DO prepare ahead of time. It's important to be ready to answer the interviewer's questions promptly. You don't want to be caught off guard. If possible, write up questions and submit them for the interview. If this isn't possible, ask for a list of the questions or topics that will be covered.

DON'T take over. Let the interviewer ask the questions and control the flow of conversation. It's not your show—you're a guest. Let the interviewer set the tone. Write down a couple of topics you want to be sure are mentioned, and find a good opportunity to bring them up. Leave the audience wanting to know more.

DO breathe. Take your time; pause when you can. You want to be heard, not leave people scratching their heads when you're finished. Focus on answering the questions as simply and clearly as possible.

DON'T be a know-it-all. Yes, you may be an expert on your topic, but you don't want the listeners to be turned off by your attitude. Be professional, but be humble, and try to make it personal. If listeners can relate to you, they'll be more interested in what you have to say.

DO smile. Even if the interview is on the radio, listeners can "hear" a smile. They can tell if you're enjoying the interview or if you're shaking in your boots. Start out with a smile, and you'll enjoy the whole experience more.

DON'T panic. Everyone gets nervous, and everyone makes mistakes. If you flub up what you're saying, take a quick breath and start again. Move on as if nothing happened, and no one will even remember.

Working from home can be wonderful, but it does not always provide the experience necessary to make one comfortable with public speaking. With a little practice and these simple tips, you'll be a star in no time.

> Do not let this Book of the Law depart from your mouth; meditate on it day and night, so that you may be careful to do everything written in it. Then you will be prosperous and successful *(Joshua 1:8)*.

Live Internet Radio Shows

Another trend is live Internet radio shows. Shows like these allow listeners to tune in live and chat as well as find archived shows online. Some sources for these types of shows include BlogTalkRadio.com and TalkShoe.com. A *Washington Post* article dated March 24, 2008, titled "With BlogTalkRadio, the Commentary Universe Expands," explains just how popular these shows are becoming. The article states, "A year and a half after New Jersey businessman Alan Levy launched the venture, BlogTalkRadio is averaging 2.4 million listeners each month for programs that range from politics to the paranormal, along with sports, finance, food, religion, and romance. The Pentagon recently started two shows on the network."

Jill and Diana's show on <http://www.blogtalkradio.com>, "The CWAHM Network," has brought them a whole new way of connecting with moms. It has also given them a platform to share the success stories of other entrepreneur moms.

What's a Teleseminar?
By Randy Ingermanson

A teleseminar is a conference call for sharing information by phone. You don't need fancy equipment for a teleseminar. All you need is a telephone—and you may not even need that.

Let me explain the *why* of a teleseminar before I explain the *how*.

The whole reason for doing a teleseminar is to make it easy for public speakers to speak to large numbers of people at the same time by phone, instead of having to travel. That cuts the costs way down, because then the only costs are the long-distance fees you pay to the phone company. And it saves huge amounts of time, because nobody has to travel.

That's the *why*. Now I'll talk about the *how*.

A teleseminar is nothing but a huge conference call on the telephone. It's a live event with a host and a guest speaker. You don't have to know how it works. The phone company takes care of all the pesky details. All you have to know is how to enter a phone number.

When you register for a teleseminar on my web site, you immediately get back an e-mail with three pieces of information:

- The time and date to call.
- The long-distance phone number to call.
- An access code that lets you into the conference.

At the appointed time for the teleseminar, you enter the phone number. Then you'll hear a message asking you for the access code. You punch in the numbers for the access code and—you're in! The host takes care of everything else. All you have to do is listen. Usually the host will mute your phone so that if your dog barks, the other zillion people on the call won't hear it.

Usually the phone number for the teleseminar is a long distance call for you, so you do have to pay the toll charge for that. But that's almost always far cheaper than the cost to travel to hear a speaker—not to mention that your time is valuable, and time spent traveling is time taken from your life. With a teleseminar, you don't spend one second traveling. You just kick back at home and listen.

Attending Teleseminars

Teleseminars are a great way to learn from experts without leaving the comfort of your home. No travel expenses, jet lag, or cafeteria food makes them the perfect way for work-at-home moms to expand their business knowledge and skills.

More and more experts and authors are offering teleseminars on topics such as business, marketing, advertising, and more. Many of these subjects are of interest, but can we as business owners really learn enough to make it worth the time and expense? In short, yes. However, there are a few important steps you should take when considering a teleseminar.

Make sure the speaker is qualified. It's fairly simple to set up a teleseminar, and just about anyone could put one together. Before investing in a seminar, do some quick research on the speaker or speakers to be sure they're experienced in the topics they'll be speaking on. Search for their names using a search engine such as Google or Yahoo, and see what results are returned. Also, if they've authored a book, take a look on Amazon and read any reviews or comments posted there.

Take notes. If you're like most work-at-home moms, you have multiple projects on your mind plus keeping up with your children, spouse, and so on. In order to retain the information given during a teleseminar, don't just sit and soak it up. Make the effort to listen closely and take notes. You'll remember more of what was discussed, and you'll be able to refer to your notes in the future if necessary.

Speak up. A teleseminar is similar to a massive conference call with one main speaker. Because of the size and the virtual setting, many people feel unsure about speaking up and asking questions. However, you'll do yourself and the speaker a favor by voicing your thoughts when appropriate and asking honest questions. Chances are good that others in the group have the same questions and will appreciate your speaking up. Do be careful not to ask too many questions. This isn't a personal training session just for you, and if too many questions are asked, especially by the same person, the speaker doesn't get to cover all the material he or she has planned to share.

One good way to get the most out of a seminar is to take it with a friend. If you have a friend or colleague who's interested, you can both participate in the teleseminar, and it will give you a great topic for discussion afterwards. You will learn as much from discussions post-seminar as you will listening to the lecture. Talking it over with another attendee helps process the information and see how it applies to daily life and business.

Follow up. If a teleseminar is especially helpful to you, send a thank-you to the speaker. Try to send a written note, but if that isn't possible, an e-mail will do. By making contact with the speaker and showing your appreciation, you'll not only provide encouragement—you'll also be networking. You never know what type of response you might receive, and you may even make a new friend or find a mentor.

The key to getting the most out of teleseminars is to find the ones that are given by experts in their field and that interest you the most. The next time you find a teleseminar that catches your interest, grab your pen and paper, and tune in. If you can find a colleague who's interested in joining you, that's even better. You'll learn more and have more fun in the process.

May the LORD make you increase, both you and your children *(Psalm 115:14).*

Blogging

The term *blog* is short for "web log," which just means an online journal or log. You can jot down personal thoughts and notes, post articles you've written, or keep track of interesting web sites you find. A blog is something entirely of your own creation, and you can use it to share your thoughts with the world. At least, that's with those who find it. Plus, it's an excellent way to promote your business.

These are many ways to create a blog. The easiest by far is to use one of the tools available online, such as Google's Blogger. You can create your blog for free using their online tools and templates. There's nothing to download. After you've created the blog, you can then publish your blog through Google, and your blog is posted online for others to find.

Jill's choice, which is a little more involved than Blogger but worth the effort, is Wordpress. Wordpress can be installed wherever you store your files within your hosting account. It can then be configured using an editable theme. Wordpress is free, and there are thousands of themes to choose from. You'll need to spend some time learning the how-to of using Wordpress, but in the end you'll have an interactive web site that can grow with your business.

We're seeing more and more businesses use WordPress. It's interactive, can be updated easily, and looks good.

You must decide if your blog is going to be for business or personal use and keep the two separate. Many people do have both, but keep in mind that your clients can also see your personal blog, so post accordingly. Your personal blog can be full of thoughts and comments speaking for only yourself and maybe your family. Your business blog can be filled with articles, tips, and expert advice on your business topic.

If you want your blog to be found by others, blogging experts recommend that you begin by setting the title and descriptions for your blog. These are similar to the title and descriptions you set for your web site. Try to make them meaningful, because they're what people will see when your blog is returned in a search engine. If your description is simply "my blog," you may not draw the attention you would like.

You want to wisely use the words and links in your blogs. This is the time to get those keywords in there. Try to avoid the *click here* link. Instead, opt for links within descriptive sentences. Add the HTML link within the sentence, and attach it to the words that are closely related to the page or site you're linking to. Blog readers know when they hover over words and see the underline appear that this means it's a link. However, don't insult their intelligence with fifty "click here" links cluttering the page. As an example, to link to my web site I would say, "Please visit Christian Work at Home Moms for home-based work resources."

One of the main debates going on about blogs is whether blogging can be done to improve search engine rankings for businesses or to create a buzz about business web sites. Both of these can be true if the blog is used correctly. Many resources show that once a blog is created, many times it's listed in search engines within 48 hours. This was true of the blog I created for Christian

Work at Home Moms, <http://cwahmjill.blogspot.com>. Another advantage is that your keywords also appear in Google.

There are many ways to get your blogs noticed outside of optimizing them for search engines. For instance, there are entire web site directories devoted to listing blogs dedicated to any topic you can think of.

You can also use free tools such as FeedBurner to track the traffic on your blog and to create a dynamic title box that can be used to display your blog headlines on your web site or even in your e-mail signature. Each time you update your blog, these headlines are instantly updated.

Another great way to get your blog in front of others is to leave comments on blogs that you visit. Jill loves to check out the blogs of authors, Christian leaders, and others. When something interests her, she posts a note with her opinion or encouragement. At the end of each post she adds her name and the link to her web site:

Sincerely,

Jill Hart

Christian Work at Home Moms at <www.cwahm.com>

A good tip is to write a personal thank-you, either by e-mail or on your blog, when someone posts on your blog.

When blogging, it's best to divide your postings into categories, and most blogging software allows you to easily do this. That way, when someone comes to your blog, the person can look to the category he or she is most interested in and read your blogs on that topic.

One way blogs are used creatively in the business world is *blog tours.* A blog tour is somewhat like a book tour, but instead of going from store to store, one goes from blog to blog. This is a great concept, because it allows authors who may reach only a few hundred people at most at a book signing in a brick-and-mortar bookstore to potentially reach thousands—even millions—by doing a tour online. For example, authors who are working on promoting a book appear on a series of blogs for a few days each and make a tour of various blogs to interact with their readers.

RSS

RSS is a common term on the Internet that stands for *really simple syndication.* Jill loves RSS, because she can use Google Reader to receive that day's content from the blogs and web sites with an RSS feed. The only requirement, and it's free, is to subscribe to the RSS feeds of your choosing.

Diana's blogs are available as an RSS feed. What this means is that instead of going to their sites each day to find any new content, you would receive any new posts in Google Reader or via e-mail. CWAHM and CWAHD.com are both formatted so that all new content is available in RSS.

Quoting Jill's husband, Allen, again, here's the simplest definition of RSS: "RSS is a standard that helps define how the raw data behind a web site should look. RSS formats text so that we don't just see one massive mound of letters—we see sentences and paragraphs condensed from all that's on that web page."

To put it in layman's terms, RSS provides web content or summaries of web content together with links to the full ver-sions of the content. RSS delivers this information as an XML file called an RSS feed. This feed aids syndication and allows a web site's frequent readers to track updates on the site.

How to Use RSS

In order to receive updates from a web site using RSS, one must use an RSS reader—also known as an aggregator. There are many different RSS readers to choose from, the most popular being MyYahoo and Google Reader, and the list is ever-changing.

Most blogs include an RSS feed so that you can see the updates instantly. Look for the following symbol to identify an RSS feed.

Right-click on the symbol, and copy the link to the RSS feed. This link can then be pasted into your RSS reader to subscribe to that feed.

You may be wondering how this can benefit your business. There are four ways RSS can be useful to your business.

First, RSS allows you to get information quickly. You can find RSS feeds on topics that interest you, topics that affect your business, such as marketing tips, trends, and news, and you will be notified each and every time one of the RSS feeds is updated.

Second, you can give information to others very quickly. The CWAHM RSS feed includes articles written by Jill and other tips and tidbits about working from home. If you write or have frequent product updates, RSS is a great way to get the word out.

The third way that you can use RSS to your advantage is to use RSS content on your web site. You can add your own RSS feed on to your web site or find an RSS feed that flows well with the information you want presented on your site. Because RSS feeds update automatically, this is an easy way to keep the information on your web site fresh and ever-changing. Also, if you are already blogging, you can use RSS to integrate your blog with your web site.

Fourth, it will keep your business on the cutting edge. RSS is continually improving, and there are always new tools being developed for its use. It's always hard to adjust to new technologies, but it's important to take the plunge and learn as much as you can to see if it might benefit your business.

Contests

A contest is an easy way to build traffic on your web site. You can run a contest on a regular basis, which helps to keep regular traffic to your site. On CWAHM we run a monthly contest to build traffic and bless our visitors. We also run contests for the major holidays and for our radio broadcast.

It's best to find donations of prizes that would be of interest to your visitors. The better the prize, the more traffic you'll receive. You can also gain exposure by donating a prize. It's a win-win situation, because as a business donating a prize, you gain exposure from the contest as well.

Once you have the contest all set up, market it. Once the word starts spreading, you'll see the benefits. You can also require the visitor to do or purchase something to gain an entry to the contest. This could be a purchase or even just asking him or her to sign up for your newsletter. This helps grow your e-mail list.

As CWAHM has grown, so have the contests. Jill has been able to partner with companies such as Motive Entertainment for giveaways of products such as Ben Stein's movie *Expelled* and *The Ten Commandments* animated film. Contests like these are great ways to increase traffic to your site and bring those people back on a regular basis.

Holiday Promotions

Another low-cost way to market your business is to make the most of the holidays. One of the things we recommend doing during the holidays is showing your clients that you appreciate them. For example, on Valentine's Day you can visit local clients and drop off heart-shaped candies with cute sayings on them or Valentine cards that your kids have designed. Or you can include the candy or cards in deliveries to them. Many professionals don't receive those cute little Valentine cards that say "Be Mine" anymore, and what a hit that could be!

Also, this is a great opportunity to approach local businesses you want to target as you come bearing gifts. Of course, it's important to consider the type of business and determine if this would be well received or not.

Recently we put our heads together to think of ways to use Valentine's Day to promote our cohosted podcast. Diana came up with the idea of asking listeners to call in, give a brief description of their business, and leave a short Valentine message for their loved ones. Together we wrote a press release and sent it out online and to our local communities.

We had an overwhelming response. Over thirty moms—and one dad—called in, including a mom from Australia. Jill was interviewed live on the morning show of her local news station, and our podcast got mentions across the Internet. In addition to our podcast getting international attention, the moms—and the one dad—who took the time to call in received promotion for their businesses. Many of them took advantage of the attention by offering specials and deals for new customers who found them through the podcast. It worked.

Something else we recommend is organizing a giveaway for holidays. Diana often offers a free press release or a "free hour of submissions" as gifts to her clients. This is usually very well received. You can also donate services or products to those hosting holiday events.

Holiday marketing is great for those who offer products that could be marketed to specific groups. For example, if you have a product geared toward moms and would make a great Mother's Day gift, get busy on publicity with the Mother's Day angle.

Depending on your business, see how creative you can be when thinking of ideas for holiday promotions. A lot will depend on the type of business you run, but try to incorporate your products or services in a unique way. You never know what type of attention you might attract. For example, Diana is able to utilize different special days such as Administrative Professional Day to advertise her books or "Work in Your Bathrobe Day" for media exposure.

Web Site Visibility

An entire section in this book is devoted to your web site, but we also wanted to highlight the importance of your web site when it comes to marketing. It's not enough just to have a web presence; you must let others know your site exists. As noted earlier, one way to drive traffic to your site is through a link in your signature line. This makes it easy for the person to click on the link and go directly to your site. Then you get the opportunity to sell yourself and let people know what you do.

Most message boards allow signature lines on their boards even if they don't allow advertising. Here you will get the opportunity to list your web site and a brief description of your business or your slogan. Check the board's guidelines, and try not to get carried away or make it sound too much like an ad.

Your web site will also get visibility through the many articles you write and the places you frequent online with your social networking activities. And, of course, the keywords used bring more exposure.

Search Engine Optimization as a Marketing Tool

Search engine optimization (SEO) is effectively using keywords and keyword phrases as well as other methods to get your site recognized in the major search engines. Search engines, such as Google and Yahoo, are a great way to get traffic. There are many techniques you can utilize to help build your search engine ranking.

One technique is to concentrate on building links to your site. The more web sites that link to your web site, the higher your search engine ranking will be. If you would like to see a full listing of all of the web sites that link to you, Yahoo has a tool called "Yahoo! Site Explorer" that you can use to do just that: <https://siteexplorer.search.yahoo.com>.

It's also important to include the right keywords, meta tags, and descriptive phrases. SEO can be a book in itself, so we recommend that you learn as much as you can to do this effectively. Know your target audience, and include keywords you know they type into the major search engines to find your products.

Local Exposure and Direct Mail

Some businesses today don't realize how important direct mail is. Sending letters or other promotional material out to potential clients can be an effective marketing tool. However, you must make sure your letter gets the recognition it deserves. Here are some things to consider:

- Is your letter interesting enough that people will read it?
- Will they read the whole letter? Word it so they don't pick up a line or two in each paragraph and skim over the rest of the paragraph.
- Do you have a "call to action" so they know what you want them to do after receiving this letter, such as calling you or going to your web site?
- Do you leave a lasting impression? When those who have read your letter see your name again, will they remember that letter, or when they have a need for your services, will they contact you?

Direct mail can also be a great way to say thank you. Gather the mailing addresses of your customers so you can send a handwritten thank-you note after they make purchases. If possible, include a pen, magnet, or other marketing material that will continually remind them of you and your business. When you receive a little promotional item in the mail, such as a magnet, do you usually keep it? Most of these items end up on desks or refrigerators.

Don't forget to follow up. It's important to keep in contact and send multiple mailings so your recipients become familiar with your name and business.

Exchanging Links

You can also market your business by exchanging links with other web sites. Search for and contact web sites that offer content similar to yours. Offer them a link on your web site in exchange for their linking to you. This is a great way to gain links to your web site and get a better search engine position. Just make sure to personalize your response.

Paid Advertising

Paid advertising, which can be paying for a text or graphic ad on a web site or in a magazine, in addition to many other means, can be an easy way to market your business whether you're just starting out or are already to the point that you're ready to take your business to the next level. However, don't expect miracles. Plan to advertise for a month or two before deciding whether or not your ad is getting results. It takes time to build a presence and for people to take action. You may also need to try several different types of ads and wording to see what works best for you.

Buttons and Banners

Button and banner online advertising gets your business directly in front of your target audience at a reasonable rate. Many web sites and blogs offer banner advertising or will exchange banner ads with you.

Keep in mind that this is an important part of your business image, as people will begin to recognize you by this means. Buttons and banners come in many shapes and sizes; however, the standard button is square in shape—125 x 125 pixels—and the standard banner is rectangular in shape—468 x 60 pixels.

Many people don't understand the difference between a button and a banner. The main distinction is the shape. When advertising with a button or banner, pay close attention to the requirements for the ads you are purchasing. Make note of the size of the button or banner requested as well as the maximum file size allowed.

When looking into button or banner advertising, you'll often find the terms *animated* and *static*. A static ad is a button or banner that does not move. An animated button will have more than one frame. It may have text that rotates, a picture that moves, or other animated effects.

If you would like a custom button or banner with wording and graphics specific to your business, Jill offers custom button and banner creation on CWAHM.com. Consider an animated button or banner that allows you to provide more information in the same amount of space. CWAHM also offers a limited number of free-to-use general work-at-home banners and buttons for moms with a limited advertising budget. Below you'll find examples of banners and buttons that Jill has created.

Yellow Pages and Christian Directories

For many businesses, an ad in the Yellow Pages or a Christian directory can be very effective. Many virtual assistants advertise this way and find it successful. Diana had an ad in the Yellow Pages for many years for her word processing business. She discovered that she did get a lot of responses, but many clients were looking for same-day turnarounds or small assignments. The good news is that small assignments often turned into full-time clients, so it was worth it. Also, she was able to get a listing by just having a business line installed, so the cost was kept to a minimum.

Christian directories can work well too. Many Christians want to work with other Christians and look in a Christian directory first. They believe that a Christian-based business will be more ethical and honest. We also discovered that many Christian businesses keep a supply of these directories on hand for their customers, and that opens the door to more customers.

The key to success is to research the directories and make sure they're legitimate and will provide the exposure you're seeking while matching the target audience with your products or services.

Newspaper and Magazine Advertising

Newspaper and magazine advertising may or may not be a viable marketing option for your business. Diana discovered that it can be very successful if you target the right publications, so be sure that the publication's readership includes your target market. Ask for statistics and distribution numbers so that you'll know what type of reach your ad will receive.

Diana provides a good example of a successful magazine ad when she advertised in *Home Business* magazine. For approximately $80 she was able to get a classified ad in this reputable publication. The results were excellent.

If you're thinking of advertising in a newspaper, check the publications prior to placing your ad to see what other business are advertising in the newspaper. Check the newspaper for a few weeks in a row to determine if those advertisers are consistently marketing in this publication. If the same ads are in the newspaper week after week, that's an indication that the businesses are having success with their ads.

Look for the best rates, the best newspapers and magazines, and most important, the best bang for your buck. Look for business promotions. Newspapers will often have an annual or biannual business networking section. It's extremely important to be consistent when you advertise. People need to get familiar with you and see your name mentioned more than once.

Client Referrals and Word-of-Mouth Advertising

Happy, satisfied clients are like money in the bank—that is, the money you *aren't* paying for additional marketing because those satisfied clients are spreading the word about you and your services. Every time you get a referral, put a dollar amount to it, because that's what it truly represents.

It's important that potential clients see those referrals. We recommend putting them on your web site, in your portfolio or proposal, and having them available when potential clients ask.

Also, with the rise in social networking, there's more opportunity for those clients to write testimonials for you that others will see. Encourage your clients to do so by providing the link and making it easy to do. Also, let your clients know that you're active on these social networking sites. You can simply add a link to your signature to show which ones they can find you on.

Word of mouth is similar. The clients might not write testimonials, but they tell others, and that's priceless. Many feel better working with someone who has been recommended, especially online. Let clients know that you appreciate word-of-mouth referrals. Also, it helps to show your appreciation. Even a personal thank-you card is appreciated, but you can do more. A gift certificate to Amazon or Starbucks is a great idea.

Seeking Product Reviews

One excellent way to get exposure for your business is to get reviews. This works for books and products, and Diana incorporates this method in several clients' publicity campaigns in addition to the marketing of her own books. It really works.

Cher Klosner Lane is a fabulous musician and has several CDs out. Among many other marketing methods, she utilizes getting reviews as one of her top marketing tools. Here's what she has to say about the importance of reviews.

When my brother, Gene, and I released our fourth CD, *Stardust,* a two-disc lullaby collection for all ages, we were entering new territory—the children's market. Prior to releasing *Stardust,* we had built a loyal mailing list of close to 10,000 names by performing at festivals, colleges, and churches. With *Stardust,* however, we knew we had a CD that went beyond our mailing list—a CD that could be in the hands of all parents who have ever had trouble putting their children to sleep or have had to endure listening to obnoxious children's CDs that make them want to pull their hair out.

So where would we start? A commercial! We considered a big, national, sixty-second spot that would play snippets of our music. How ideal! We met with an ad agency, and my lofty dreams of a national commercial were quickly grounded; just a simple, thirty-second, locally targeted commercial was going to cost tens of thousands of dollars.

What next? We had to think like a first-time mom. When my son was first born, I looked to parent publications for advice, to find out the latest recalls, and to find the latest and greatest products. So we contacted many parent publications for advertising rates but quickly realized that the traditional print advertising route was way beyond our allotted advertising budget. Once again, we had to think like a mom. What would persuade a parent to buy one product over another? It boiled down to two things: word of mouth—what other parents would recommend—and seeing products that had won parent awards and earned the seals of approval.

I had seen them a hundred times, that little sticker on a product that screams, "Hey, Mom! Rest assured this product has been parent tested and parent approved. You have our word on it. And we have a nice, shiny sticker to prove it." I remember seeing a framed recording hanging on the wall in the studio where we recorded our second CD. Right beside the framed recording was a framed parenting award certificate. I thought, *Wow! It must be good.* If it persuaded me, I knew it would persuade others.

I asked other moms if the stickers ever helped them make buying decisions. Over seventy-five percent of the moms I asked were more inclined to buy products that had that sticker. That was enough for me to look into the process.

I was pleased to find several reputable companies that give the awards. There were submission fees, and if your product wins an award, the stickers cost extra as well. But not every product submitted wins an award. Every product is put through rigorous testing methods, and a product truly has to earn the award. If it doesn't meet the standard set by the company, it's out of the contest. On the other hand, if you're a lucky recipient of an award, it's yours to keep. And it *does* carry weight. We have had several articles and news stories printed about us simply because we won an award. In addition, the award companies promote their winners as well. The return on investment is worth it.

I ran a very unscientific study comparing our sales at one store in which we were not advertising. The sales tripled after we went in and put the stickers on the CD. Could be a fluke, but it was enough to make me glad we went through the awards process. And we're going to go through it again with other companies. One can never have too many awards. Don't you agree? On top of that, the reviews and comments made about our product during the testing period were sent to us to use. And a good review can get you a lot of mileage.

If you don't like taking risks, or you don't have thick skin, you're in the wrong business, and you won't like the product review process. But if you really believe in your product, as I do, and you're willing to take the good with the bad, as I am, sending your product out to the world to be judged is the greatest form of free advertising. It's that second factor of what would persuade me to buy a product—word of mouth, what other parents had to say.

In the beginning I felt completely lost. I was blindly sending off CDs to every company that did reviews, always wondering, *Just who are these people? Does anyone even read or care what they have to say?* Thankfully, an entrepreneur friend of mine, who was much more experienced at this than me, explained tool bars and site rankings. Finally—the piece of the puzzle I had been missing. The site ranking gave me an indication of how much traffic a particular site gets, therefore, how many would read their review of my product. The light went on, and I got it. I have now become much more site-savvy and send products only to sites that have a great rating or are of special interest to my particular product, which in my case are children's music review blogs.

Is it a lot of work? You bet. Is it scary to think you might not get a great review? Sure it is. Will all of the reviews be good? There are no guarantees. But so what if you do get an occasional clunker? It's one person's opinion. Move forward and think of all the great reviews you're bound to get elsewhere. Then use those reviews that make you and your product shine!

—Cher Klosner Lane
Singer and songwriter
Co-founder of Audible Chocolate Productions
<www.stardustlullaby.com>

Business Expos and Job Fairs

Many home-based workers participate in job fairs and business expos. They can be fabulous for business—at least for the right business. If you decide to get a booth at an expo, it's important to do your homework and know that your target audience will be there. If not, you'll stand out like a sore thumb and will have wasted a chunk of your hard-earned money.

There are numerous expos you can look into, including business gatherings in your local community and local chamber of commerce events. These events are usually advertised in the local paper well in advance. You can also get on the mailing list to be notified of upcoming events or find this information online at message boards of your peers. Businesses often discuss upcoming events on the boards.

Be prepared. Do you have an adequate supply of business cards, flyers, magnets, books, products? Remember to hand out something unique for attendees to take home with them to remember you by.

Business expos are also great for adding to your sales force. They're a great resource if you're in direct sales or have a product of your own and need to increase sales. You'll have the ability to visit with a diverse group of people, and you'll find people who enjoy sales and want to join your team.

Business Mentoring Groups

Finding a mentor can be a great way to build your business and make contacts in your field. We had the privilege of interviewing Kelly McCausey, co-founder of MomMasterminds (<www.mommasterminds.com>).

We asked Kelly to tell us about MomMasterminds.

Kelly: MomMasterminds is a private mentoring community for moms who want to learn how to apply Internet marketing principles to their businesses. They get access to a huge amount of learning resources, including printable ebooks, audios, and videos covering topics like building a web site, how to write compelling web copy, and how to optimize your web site for the search engines—honestly and ethically—with an eye for the long term. New resources are added every single month so the information is always fresh and up to date.

It includes a members-only forum where everyone can ask questions, get feedback, and brainstorm business ideas. Many profitable partnerships have been born on these boards.

We asked Kelly how it all began.

Kelly: Alice Seba of Internet Based Moms approached me with the idea of creating a private membership site for moms who are really serious about learning the right way to build a profitable business. I was excited to partner with her on the project. We launched in the summer of 2004 and had great success with it.

We asked Kelly what tips she shares with moms who are trying to make their way in the home-business world.

Kelly: Seek out moms who have been around longer and are experiencing the success that you want to achieve for yourself. It's important to choose mentors who share your values and goals. Be careful about listening to the crowd; they can lead you astray. What is popular at the moment may not be profitable long-term.

A generous man will prosper; he who refreshes others will himself be refreshed (*Proverbs 11:25*).

6 BUSINESS NUTS AND BOLTS

When we began our businesses we both had dreams of what life would be like as successful entrepreneurs. However, as our businesses grew, each of us learned that there were many details to be addressed on a regular basis that had nothing to do with the dream.

Success or failure is in the details. Ignore the nuts and bolts of running a business, and nothing else will run smoothly. But pay special attention to them, and you'll have a more successful and smoothly operating business.

Bookkeeping and Record-keeping

Choosing how you'll run your business is as important as choosing your business. It's imperative that before you put out the open sign you sit down and map out how you'll keep track of your business finances. You may think that you won't make enough for it to matter in the early days, but the truth is that it *does* matter. Irresponsibility in this area can seriously hinder your business in the future.

Bookkeeping must be done consistently throughout the year. If you're a procrastinator, you must either find a way to hold yourself accountable for your bookkeeping or hire someone to take care of it for you. If bookwork isn't tended to regularly, it will quickly become a burden as accounts receivable and accounts payable pile up. If you make more than you anticipated, you could face additional taxes due that could have been planned for had you kept track of your books throughout the year. If you're on top of things all year long, you may realize in September that you need more deductions, and you can go ahead and buy supplies ahead of time, upgrade your computer, and so on.

Decide which software to use for your bookkeeping. Some of the more popular ones are Quickbooks and Peachtree. It's important to choose the one that fits your business. Jill made the mistake of keeping all her records originally in an Excel spreadsheet. This worked well at first, but as CWAHM grew, she found herself in need of both bookkeeping software and a bookkeeper. She had to spend hours inputting past sales and expenses in order for the software to be accurate for that year. It was a major headache that could have been avoided by using the right software from the beginning. As always, hindsight is 20/20.

You must keep records that the Internal Revenue Service can use that will verify income and expenses. We recommend keeping the following: receipts, bank statements, business credit card statements, business bills and payments, and so on.

One way to stay organized is to invest in an expandable file folder—a good-quality one that will allow you to separate everything upon receipt. Diana separates her bank statements, postage receipts, subcontractor's statements, office supplies, phone bills, and anything else business-related. Everything she needs at the end of the year is right there, and if she needs to find something throughout the year, it's right at her fingertips. A filing cabinet works very well if you have the space available.

Learn the best ways to do things. For example, if you use QuickBooks, you can download your PayPal account and bank statements. Seek advice from peers in your industry who can give you advice on finding an easy, workable method.

We're happy to give you up-to-date information as to what's worked for us, but the bookkeeping for your business is your responsibility. While it will be helpful to you to know how other home-based business owners handle the nuts-and-bolts issues, our best advice to you is to enlist the services of an accountant or attorney for your bookkeeping and legal issues.

Business Checking Account

Setting up a separate checking account for your business may not seem like a pressing matter, but it's actually an important aspect of organizing your home-based business. In fact, if you're beginning a direct sales business, it will more than likely be a requirement that you have a separate checking account before you can start. It's essential to keep your personal and business accounts totally separate.

Then I realized that it is good and proper for a man to eat and drink, and to find satisfaction in his toilsome labor under the sun during the few days of life God has given him—for this is his lot. Moreover, when God gives any man wealth and possessions, and enables him to enjoy them, to accept his lot and be happy in his work—this is a gift of God *(Ecclesiastes 5:18-19)*.

Tax Preparation

Here a few tax-time tips:

- **Report all income.** Accurately report all your taxable income.
- **Itemize all expenses and deductions.** Break these down into the appropriate categories.
- **Save receipts.** When itemizing your deductions, you must have a paper trail of them.
- **Make sure all deductions are legitimate.** You won't have to worry about an audit if you're honest and have filed your taxes correctly.

- **Prepare your taxes with care.** Arithmetic errors draw the attention of the IRS. Also, be neat if you do your taxes by hand so that your return can be read.

- **Have a professional fill out your forms.** It's worth the peace of mind to make sure your taxes are done correctly. Remember: you can save a lot of money if you take the proper deductions.

- **Sign your form.** Unsigned tax returns raise an automatic red flag. You're probably thinking this is a no-brainer, but it happens frequently.

- **File electronically.** The IRS actually prefers this, because it saves work on their end.

It's important to include all deductions and to keep up with the latest tax laws and changes. For example, the mileage deduction often changes in favor of business owners. If you do a lot of traveling, that can make a substantial difference. Even if you don't do a lot of traveling, it's extra money in your pocket.

Following is information we learned from Jackie Perlman, CPA and lead researcher for The Tax Institute at H&R Block. We asked her for two tips she could provide to small businesses or home-based businesses on what can make preparing taxes a little easier.

Jackie: Have all your books and records organized and ready for review: invoices, checks, receipts, billing statements, bank statements, and so on. If you use computer software to keep records, make sure your tax preparer has the latest record—probably December 31.

We asked Jackie to tell us what she thinks is the biggest mistake most home-based businesses or small businesses make in tax preparation.

Jackie: Not keeping separate records for business and personal items. Your business should have a separate checking account and credit card. Your office supplies and your son's football equipment do not belong on the same statement. Running your business like a business goes a long way toward substantiating expenses and making tax preparation less intimidating.

We hear of mistakes that the IRS sees as red flags. We don't want to raise any of those! So we asked Jackie to give us a few tips on things we should watch out for.

Jackie: Make sure that every expense is substantiated with a receipt or record. It's not the red flags that are the problem. If you have a large expenditure that has a legitimate business purpose and you can substantiate the expense, it is wrong not to claim the expense just because it might make the IRS take notice. Very often expenses are denied because the business owner cannot substantiate them, not because the items were nondeductible.

We asked Jackie if there were any comical experiences she would like to share with our readers.

Jackie: Sorry, but the only thing I can think of is Richard Hatch going on national television and stating that he paid no tax on his winnings from "Survivor."

It's imperative that you communicate with your accountant throughout the year. Jill learned this the hard way. In one year CWAHM.com tripled in both size and income. What a blessing! Unfortunately, the accountant had estimated only a small growth in income for that year. The taxes owed were overwhelming. Thankfully, once deductions and expenses were calculated, it wasn't as bad as it originally seemed. This could have been avoided if Jill and her accountant had communicated regularly throughout the year.

Here's what Jill has to say about her experience:

After the frustrations with the first two accountants, I searched until I found an accountant I could both trust and afford. I send the accountant quarterly statements so that the growth of my business is documented and necessary changes to my tax estimates can be made.

I've also hired a bookkeeper and have begun using QuickBooks to track all income and expenses. I use the online version of QuickBooks, because for a small monthly fee, it allows me to have access from multiple locations. I can log on from my home office, my bookkeeper can log in from her office, and our accountant has his own log-in as well. This also eliminates the worry of losing data. If any of our computers crash, we know that our financial data is online as well as backed up, so there's no concern over data loss.

I also incorporated the business at the suggestion of my accountant and attorney. This affords structure to help produce business growth, tax deductions, and an amount of legal protection under the corporate entity.

The great part about mistakes like the one Jill made with estimated taxes is that we can all learn from the experiences of others. Choosing an accountant is a very important decision and not one you should take lightly. Ask your friends and colleagues for referrals to accountants they have used and been satisfied with. Take the time to speak with multiple accountants to get a feel for who might be best suited to handle your business needs. You can also check with the Better Business Bureau before you sign a contract with an accounting firm—or with any other contracted labor—to make sure there are no unresolved complaints on file.

Also, keep in mind that setting out to find an accountant on April 10 is not the best time. Build a relationship with your accountant so he or she knows you and your business and family and then will be able to spot deductions you might have missed. Find someone you trust who can advise you on some of these tough decisions. It's imperative to know all the facts before you take steps such as incorporating. Questions like these need to be addressed to a financial or legal professional.

Lesley Johnson, CPA, of Johnson Financial Services offers the following tips:

Many small business owners are unaware of the tax aspects of their business or just assume that their accountant will figure it out for them on April 15. Inadequate records could also cost you eligible tax savings and create many headaches. The most commonly missed tax savings opportunities are the home office deduction, business mileage expenses, and expenses for meals and entertainment. The most confusing issues for small business owners are employment taxes, self-employment taxes, and how to determine the status of an independent contractor. To avoid costly problems, tax planning needs to be done throughout the year. Year-round financial planning for your small business is crucial for survival and growth.

What Type of Business to Form?

The vast majority of home-based businesses are set up as sole proprietorships. It can be the simplest setup with the least work required to get established. A sole proprietorship is solely responsible for the decisions and management of the business. To start a sole proprietorship, you simply start doing business under your business name. There are no legalities to form a sole proprietorship as there are in forming a corporation.

Other business types include a partnership, a corporation, an S corporation, or a limited liability company (LLC). S Corporations are used by several home-based businesses as they offer limited liability without the additional taxation of a regular corporation. We recommend that you do research online and through books to see what's best for you. Then if you're unsure of what would be the best for your business, contact your accountant, your attorney, or a SCORE (Service Corps of Retired Executives) representative for assistance.

Business Licenses

To operate a home-based business, you'll likely need to have the appropriate licenses. This varies from state to state, so we recommend that you go to your city's web site or the appropriate office.

If you have difficulty locating the appropriate place to get this information, contact your local SCORE offices, or call their main number at 800-634-0245 to obtain the local

SCORE office number for your area. To visit SCORE online, go to <http://www.score.org>. Also, the Small Business Administration (SBA) can provide you with this information. To obtain the number of the local SBA, call 800-827-5722, or visit the SBA online at <http://www.sba.gov>.

Zoning

You should also check the zoning laws to see if extra work is required. Depending upon your business type, you'll need to contact your local zoning agency to find out if you need permission to operate a business from your home. You can find the contact information for your local zoning office in the phone book or online.

Business Insurance

You should make sure that both you and your business are covered if you suffer a loss or theft. Fortunately, insurance is available for homeowners and renters.

Contact your homeowner insurance policy provider to find out what's available. Some companies offer business insurance, or you may be able to get a rider to your current policy to cover your home business, computers, and other high-dollar equipment.

Keep good records on all the equipment in your office, and keep them separate from your home listings. We recommend keeping all receipts for equipment purchases in case you need to file a claim, and we also recommend taking photographs of your present equipment and any new equipment you purchase.

It takes only a few minutes, and if something happens, you'll be in a much better position when filing a claim.

Many states require that you have additional insurance to cover your business if you'll have customers coming to your home for business purposes. Be sure to check into that if this applies to your business.

Health Insurance

Health insurance used to be something you gave up in order to work from home. Thankfully, this is no longer the case. Many companies offer health insurance for the self-employed. A few of the companies that we're aware of include

- American Family Insurance
- Blue Cross Blue Shield
- Humana

There are many others. Search online for local insurance agents that offer this service. You can also visit web sites such as <http://www.ehealthinsurance.com> and get a listing of companies in your area that offer coverage.

Many direct sales companies offer health insurance to their representatives. Check with any companies you're interested in to see if they offer insurance benefits. Here are a few we're aware of:

- Shaklee
- Avon
- Tupperware
- Taste of Home Entertaining
- BeautiControl
- Pampered Chef

Also, be sure to check into the benefits offered by any home business associations you may belong to. They often offer insurance as one of the perks.

In some cases, you may find it beneficial just to add extra coverage to your spouse's policy. Take the time to review this with your family—before you need it.

Getting Paid

Setting your rate and prices for your products can sometimes be a challenge. Take your time here, and make sure you charge what you're worth. Many businesses make the mistake of undervaluing their services or products. Do your research thoroughly, and charge accordingly. You should determine what the industry standards are for your type of business. Also, consider your own skills and expertise. If you're selling products, find competing prices. Ask folks buying the products how much they pay and whether or not they feel that's a fair price and how they came to that conclusion.

Answer these questions when setting prices for your goods or services:

- What do you bring to the table that your potential clients want and need?
- What sets you apart from others who are in the same business?
- What do you need to make each year to show a profit with your business?
- What are you worth?

We don't recommend setting your rates at rock-bottom prices to get the most work or to sell the most product. That rarely works. Businesses today want top-quality work done correctly and in a timely manner, and customers want to know the products they purchase are top-of-the-line.

> Lazy hands make a man poor, but diligent hands bring wealth (*Proverbs 10:4).*

Collecting Payment

There are many ways to collect payment. Some clients prefer electronic payments rather than going through the hassle of writing a check and mailing it. It also enables you to get payment immediately without waiting for a check to arrive.

PayPal is a popular form of paying online. It's easy to set up, accepts money from checking accounts as well as credit and debit cards, and most of your potential clients are already familiar with it. It also makes bookkeeping easier. A transaction fee is charged, but the convenience may well be worth it. If you have a large transaction, though—let's say a $3,000 retainer payment—a check would be a better option to avoid the large transaction fee.

Check your PayPal account regularly for accuracy, and record every PayPal transaction into your bank account. PayPal also converts to software programs like QuickBooks and Excel for easy bookkeeping.

Another option is to open a merchant account. ProPay is one company that offers this service. ProPay allows you to have a merchant account and accept credit cards without signing up for an account with them. There are other options as well;

many companies allow you to accept credit card payments via phone.

Speaking of credit cards, it's important to be somewhat cautious when accepting credit card payments. If something doesn't seem quite right, err on the side of caution. For example, if a company approaches you and wants to purchase 100 of your *items*, not mentioning the items by name, this is an obvious red flag. Run!

Most credit card companies allow up to six months for a fraudulent charge to be reported. In order for you, the merchant, to counteract a false report against you, you must have proof of shipping if it's a tangible product. It costs a few cents extra to add delivery confirmation or signature confirmation when shipping a package, but in the end it may save you much more.

Billing

It's important to bill clients promptly. Also, the payment arrangement must be clear in the contract. Decide when payments will be due. Options are Net 10, Net 15, Net 30, or upon receipt of bill. Basically that means in 10 days, 15 days, 30 days, or upon receipt of the bill.

Don't let clients get too far behind. If a reasonable period of time goes by and you haven't received your payment, e-mail the client or send a friendly reminder through PayPal. Be careful not to send the reminder notice too soon; a client will not appreciate getting a reminder if you just sent the bill that morning.

Your billing standards should become the norm in your business. If you make an exception for one client for "just this once," because of the client's unique circumstance, it can backfire on you. It's tempting to bend a little, but if you stick to your guns every time, your policies become set in stone, and success is sure to follow.

Diana usually works on a retainer. In the virtual assisting industry, this is common. Her clients retain her services for a certain number of hours each month for a lower rate than her regular hourly rate. This ensures a regular income each and every month. It's a benefit to the clients, because they get the work at a lower hourly rate and are also guaranteed that she'll be available to do their work that month. If your business is one that could operate on retainers, it could be of benefit to you as well as your clients.

For example, let's say a virtual assistant's rate is $75 per hour. Here are some tips for a retainer basis:

$75—standard hourly rate

$65—per hour when retained twelve hours per month

$60—per hour when retained twenty-plus hours per month

Clients will often sign retainers on a three-month commitment and then sign a "Notice to Renew Retainer" at the end of that term to keep the retainer ongoing. Most retainers are paid at the start of the retainer period and billed monthly. Of course, this is just one method to set up the retainer relationship. You can also do a retainer with no minimum monthly requirements. The retainer continues monthly, and the client will provide a fifteen-day notice if he or she wishes to discontinue it.

Some clients offer their credit cards and allow you to charge their cards for the retainer amount. This is a convenience for them, as they don't have to worry about getting the payment to you. Also, it's a benefit to you as you are assured payment.

Another method of getting guaranteed payment is through regular monthly or weekly subscriptions billed through a company such as PayPal. The client is billed each month, and it's deposited automatically into your PayPal or bank account. Jill's company, CWAHM, has regular advertisers who pay by subscription each month, which helps her maintain a consistent monthly income.

Protecting Your Trademark

When Ellen Parlapiano and Patricia Cobe wrote their first Mompreneurs book in 1996, they knew they had coined a unique word to describe entrepreneurial moms. They quickly protected their clever phrasing by trademarking the word "mompreneurs" and naming their consulting company Mompreneurs, LLC. Then they began building their Mompreneurs brand—first on iVillage.com in the late 1990s and now at their independent web site, MompreneursOnline.com.

Today Cobe and Parlapiano are considered the media's go-to experts on the topic of work-from-home moms. "We have watched the mompreneurs movement explode over the last decade and are proud to be the ones who first labeled and advised this inspirational group of mothers," says Parlapiano.

As the number of work-from-home moms has grown, so has MompreneursOnline.com. The site offers bustling message boards, blogs from moms in various fields, and a Mompreneurs Marketplace featuring products and services created by mothers. Though Cobe and Parlapiano may have transformed the word "mompreneurs" into a household word, they're careful to protect their brand. "When you own a trademark, you must constantly patrol the web for any unlawful infringements," says Parlapiano. "While we're thrilled that the catchy word we coined and trademarked has become popular with others, we also must be diligent about reminding business owners and the media that only we are legally able to use the word "mompreneurs" in commerce.

Backing Up Business Information

One important thing you can do for your business is to back up your information regularly. In the blink of an eye, your computer can go on the fritz, and all is lost. You don't want to be caught in this situation with customers expecting their orders and accountants expecting your records. Don't learn this lesson the hard way. Set up a regular schedule for how and when you'll back up all your computer files and information.

You can have an external hard drive—a flash drive, a CD backup—or an online option such as Moxy or Carbonite may work best for you. It doesn't matter how you choose to back up your work as long as you do it regularly. We also feel you should use several techniques. What if your computer and backup hard drive are stolen? Wouldn't you want other options?

Just as important as backing up your computer is knowing how to retrieve that information. It differs for each backup method. We suggest restoring your information before you need it to make sure that you know how to handle the process if you did experience a computer crash.

Scheduling Your Work Day

Can a work-at-home mom really stick to a schedule? The answer is—*sometimes*. Setting a schedule for your work will benefit you, your children, and your employer or customers.

Whether you're working from home as a telecommuter or business owner, it will be important to schedule your time over the course of the week so that you'll know you have enough time set aside to get in the number of work hours required. Budget time for phone calls, carpooling, play time with your kids, and anything else that will distract you during your working hours. Be reasonable with your time, and don't expect to sit at your computer working for eight solid hours. It's important that you find a way to balance your home life with your work life. That can be very tricky when your home is also your office.

Try to set a schedule that will not overwhelm you. It's important that you keep to your schedule, especially in the first few months. Set a goal of two or three weeks, and try to stick to your schedule to meet your goal. You have probably heard that it takes twenty-one days to develop a new habit, so in this amount of time you should be able to adjust to your new schedule.

You need to set aside not only hours for you to work but also hours to be available for clients to contact you. It is, of course, important that you're available to your clients as much as possible; good customer service is one way that a home-based business can stand out from the competition. However, you must also set aside some time each day when you're *not* available to customers. This will be the time you'll focus on your family. They are, after all, the reason you're working from home in the first place. Don't develop the habit of spending every evening on the phone with clients. This can happen more quickly than you think.

It's easy to get caught up in the business of being in business and the excitement of selling goods or services. It's important to maintain a careful balance of business life and family life. Remember: success is measured in happy husbands and well-developed children. We'll be remembered for our contribution to our family, not how great we did with our businesses. If we keep an eternal perspective on things, we'll be reminded to focus on God first, our family next, and our businesses third.

> Do not store up for yourselves treasures on earth, where moth and rust destroy, and where thieves break in and steal. But store up for yourselves treasures in heaven, where moth and rust do not destroy, and where thieves do not break in and steal. For where your treasure is, there your heart will be also *(Matthew 6:19-21).*

Jill read an article not long ago that really made her think. It was a "true confession" of a mother who said that her children bore her. She stated that she never attends their school functions, children's birthday parties, and so forth. Those things are boring to her, so she sends the nanny in her place. She would rather shop or eat with friends than spend time with her children. It made Jill wonder if this type of mother is a rarity or if there are many mothers who feel this way about raising their children.

What's your attitude? Do you treasure the time you have with your children, or would you rather be elsewhere? The time we have with our little ones is a precious gift from God.

We encourage you to take time out every day to focus on your children and remind them of how much you love them.

Remember: God will provide for your needs if you are seeking Him and following His will by being at home. He will bless your efforts in both business and family. This does not mean that you'll end up with a multi-million-dollar business but that He'll provide for your *needs*.

It takes a lot of trust in God to refuse to answer the business phone line if it rings during the time you've set aside to focus on your family. God will not miss your efforts at pleasing Him. Do everything you can to assure that the clients are taken care of in advance so they won't need to reach you during this time. Often just a few changes in how you do things will allow you to set standards in place that will save time and eliminate extra steps. You know your business best; what are some steps that would work for you?

One way that Jill has found to stick to her schedule is to make lists of what needs to be done around the house and for her business. You can create a daily to-do list, a weekly to-do list, and a monthly to-do list. Your lists might look something like this:

Daily To-Do List

1. Web site updates

2. Client project

3. Laundry—Monday, Wednesday, Friday

4. Networking

5. . . .

Weekly To-Do List

1. Web site newsletter

2. Find one new free advertising opportunity

3. Vacuum and mop

4. . . .

Monthly To-Do List

1. You get the idea . . .

During more hectic months—December, for instance—Jill has been known to make up a list for every day of the week. This helps her stay organized and ensures that everything that needs to be done gets done. Many work-at-home moms use a large monthly calendar and plan out the month ahead of time. They then add to the calendar as things come up and can easily glance at it to make sure they don't double-book.

Jill has found that about every six months or so she needs to sit down and set a new schedule. As the children get older, schedules need to be revamped to meet their needs. Jill states, "Since my children are the reason I'm running a home-based business, it's important to remember that they're to be my first priority. I try to set a schedule that allows me to give my customers great customer service and quick responses, yet allows me to spend top-quality time with my kids."

Time Management

Good time management skills are extremely important. One of the biggest time-wasters for a work-at-home mom is to lose her focus. It's easy to do. Let's say you constantly check your e-mail during the day. Diana is guilty of this one. Every time she stops what she's doing and responds to an e-mail, she loses her focus.

We recommend setting aside a few times each day to check e-mail and a certain amount devoted to responding. If you have clients who need you to check your e-mail constantly, go ahead and check it, but wait to respond until the scheduled time. Inform your clients to indicate in the subject line if the e-mail needs immediate attention.

You can schedule your day in Outlook or a planner. A good way to get a handle on where your time goes is to make a copy of the following chart and put it in a notebook; then write down everything you do for an entire week. You'll be able to recognize all the little time-robbers that grab your attention during your work hours. Remember, though, that just being aware of where your time goes won't solve the problem. You have to take steps to change your patterns.

My Business Daily Log

Time	Task	Money Made	Time	Task	Money Made
12:00 AM			12:00 PM		
12:30 AM			12:30 PM		
1:00 AM			1:00 PM		
1:30 AM			1:30 PM		
2:00 AM			2:00 PM		
2:30 AM			2:30 PM		
3:00 AM			3:00 PM		
3:30 AM			3:30 PM		
4:00 AM			4:00 PM		
4:30 AM			4:30 PM		
5:00 AM			5:00 PM		
5:30 AM			5:30 PM		
6:00 AM			6:00 PM		
6:30 AM			6:30 PM		
7:00 AM			7:00 PM		
7:30 AM			7:30 PM		
8:00 AM			8:00 PM		
8:30 AM			8:30 PM		
9:00 AM			9:00 PM		

9:30 AM			9:30 PM		
10:00 AM			10:00 PM		
10:30 AM			10:30 PM		
11:00 AM			11:00 PM		
11:30 AM			11:30 PM		

Client Time Log

Client	Date	Time	Task

In order to make the best use of your time, try these tips and see if they work for you:

- *Think of time as money.* The next time you spend an extra fifteen minutes on an instant message or phone call, assign a dollar amount to that chunk of time. If you make $40 an hour, that call cost $10. Was it worth it?

- *Write it down.* Write what down? Everything. Thoughts about your next business promotion. Thoughts on how to wow your new client with additional services he or she might not know about. Notes you just received on the phone about pick-up times for the kids. Consider a spiral notebook to cut down on little pieces of paper. Date each page or entry. That will allow you to go back and look up information by date. You can use this to jot down incoming phone messages; just be sure to follow up accordingly. Also, write a separate to-do list, a list of goals, a list of motivations. And either use an electronic calendar or carry a planner to keep track of all appointments.

- *Spend some time with your thoughts.* After you get in the habit of writing down your dreams and plans, schedule a time each week or every other week to organize them into the appropriate categories, and spend some time focusing on them. You probably don't realize how much time you spend dreaming and planning. That's just part of being a business owner, and we encourage it fully. Never stop dreaming. But dreaming at the right time can help those dreams become reality. When there's work to be done, you need to stay focused on the job at hand. By jotting down your ideas, knowing you'll get back to them, you save time now and also later by not taking up time trying to remember what great idea you had last week.

- *Make a list of all the things you're involved in.* Make special note of things you're passionate about or that benefit your business. Try to cut out the things in your life that you're doing but you can't remember why you're doing them.

- *Reward yourself often.* Find something for you. When you've successfully kept your desk organized, your time managed, your clients happy, and your kids fed, smile and say, "Hey—I did it!" You'll find you want to get that feeling again, so you'll try hard the next day to accomplish things again.

It's important to accomplish as much as you can throughout the day and also to keep track of your time. In addition to using our charts for scheduling your time, invest in a timer, and start timing different projects. How long did it take you to respond to that e-mail? How long did it take you to answer that post on a message board? Will that result in sales?

As a home-based business owner, you must remember that taking time to enjoy family is important. Therefore, take control. By the way, this tip took four minutes.

Another tip is to allow a specific amount of time for certain daily activities. Set the timer for an adequate amount of time to accomplish a certain task, and then when the time sounds, stop. You may find that you can't stop completely; however, you'll be aware of the amount of time that task requires, and next time you can schedule a realistic amount of time to complete it.

Daily To-Do List

1.	
2.	
3.	
4.	
5.	
6.	
7.	
8.	
9.	
10.	

Weekly To-Do List

1.	
2.	
3.	
4.	
5.	
6.	
7.	
8.	
9.	
10.	
11.	
12.	
13.	

14.	
15.	
16.	
17.	
18.	
19.	
20.	

Monthly To-Do List

1.	
2.	
3.	
4.	
5.	
6.	
7.	
8.	
9.	
10.	
11.	
12.	
13.	
14.	
15.	
16.	
17.	
18.	
19.	
20.	
21.	
22.	
23.	
24.	
25.	
26.	
27.	
28.	
29.	
30.	
31.	
32.	
33.	

34.	
35.	
36.	
37.	
38.	
39.	
40.	

Programs are available online and also software you can use that will help you plan and organize your time. You can find one such software at <http://www.syntap.com/products_time stamp.htm>. It's free and allows you to time how long you spend on a task, including features that let you take "slack time" for a phone call or break. Times for various tasks can also be linked to an hourly charge rate for accurate billing if needed.

Wealth and riches are in his house, and his righteousness endures forever *(Psalm 112:3).*

7 CLIENT RELATIONS

If you want to be taken seriously, it's imperative that you portray professionalism in your work-from-home endeavor. In this chapter we'll touch on some areas in which your professionalism can shine in your dealings with the public.

Communication

It's important to stay in communication with your clients. As noted earlier, if a client e-mails you and you don't respond for days, he or she will feel neglected, and you'll look unprofessional. At the very least, write back and acknowledge receipt of the e-mail and give a time frame for when you'll be able to complete the work or send the order. Communication can be as simple as keeping in touch by e-mail and letting your clients know the status of their projects. It comes down to treating your clients as you yourself would want to be treated.

If your business is primarily online, it's even more important that you communicate well. Most of your clients may never meet you face to face, so all they have to go on will be your words. Their experience, whether positive or negative, will depend largely on how well you communicate.

For example, when Jill is working on the design of buttons and banners, she generally sends out an e-mail when a client makes the purchase and asks for details of what the person would like his or her banner to look like. She also gives the client a time frame for the project. Next she sends a rough draft of the banner to get the client's approval and make sure that she's proceeding in the right direction. Once any requested changes are made and approval is given, she sends the final draft with instructions on how to use the banner the person has purchased. This keeps the customer in the loop so he or she doesn't feel as if the money paid went into cyberspace with no return.

It's imperative always to communicate with your clients, especially if you're unable to finish a task. Often in the home-based community where a lot of work is done via the Internet, something comes up that prevents a task from being completed on time. If the work-at-home mom decides not to respond to her clients to let them know the status, it gives a negative impression of her and her business and also reflects negatively on the home-based community as a whole. More than once we've heard business owners say they would never again work with someone online because of being burned in past experiences. Can you see how a negative experience reflects badly on the whole community?

The right way to handle situations such as this is as follows:

1. Find a backup who can take over and complete the project. This is the best course of action.

2. If you can't find a backup, as soon as possible contact the clients and explain what's happening. You'll find that once they're aware of the situation, they're in a position to solve it. Not only will you likely retain the clients, but they'll also appreciate the fact that you stepped up to plate. Of course, this must not become a habit.

3. Offer the client solutions. For example, "I know you needed this by this date; however, I know I can have it for you by this date." Remember—this should not be normal business practice but should be used only in a real emergency.

Your customers should always be treated with the utmost respect. Try to work with them as much as possible. You'll build customer loyalty by being flexible and courteous. Making every customer feel important is a way to build loyalty and keep customers coming back and telling others about your business. Each customer should feel like your number-one client. However, remember that this is your business, and you don't need to accept unprofessional behavior or unrealistic expectations from them.

Keep it professional. Recently Diana was following up with virtual assistants looking for another subcontractor to add to her team. In talking with one virtual assistant, during the course of the initial phone call, the woman used profanity three times and also relayed in detail a story about a former client, sharing confidential information about the client, including why the relationship went sour. Speaking negatively about a former client is never a good idea, and breaching client confidentiality is completely unacceptable. Needless to say, this was not the type of team player Diana was looking for, and the position went to someone else.

Reputation

One of your most valuable business assets is your reputation. It's imperative to keep this in mind at all times. Don't tarnish your reputation by generating negative feedback from your clients. You want them to have good feeling about you and tell their friends about you.

This ensures good word-of-mouth referrals. Think about bad experiences you've had in a store or restaurant. Did you tell your friends the story? If you did, it's very possible that they may not give that place of business a chance, because they now have a negative attitude toward it. The business may never be successful in winning your friends as customers. Think how hard it would need to work to win your respect back—if that's even possible.

A much better approach is to go out of your way for every client. We're not saying you should promise them the moon, but it's important to be courteous, professional, and accommodating to each and every client. As the old saying goes, you'll catch more flies with honey than with vinegar.

When confronted with a negative situation, pray about it. That's one of the advantages Christian work-at-home moms have. We have the faith that if we turn it over to God, the answer will come.

Another valuable asset that must be guarded is your reputation for honesty. Do your very best to be up-front and honest with everyone. People will appreciate this, and it will save you stress and allow you to keep loyal customers.

> Whoever can be trusted with very little can also be trusted with much, and whoever is dishonest with very little will also be dishonest with much *(Luke 16:10).*

Dealing with customers on a regular basis can be one of the best—and worst—parts of running an at-home business. Jill says that most of the customers she deals with are wonderful, but every once in a while someone is difficult to get along with. One recent experience involved a customer who was not satisfied with anything Jill said or did.

As her frustration mounted, Jill found herself wishing she could avoid working with this person altogether. However, she came across a verse that made her think twice about her attitude:

If you love those who love you, what credit is that to you? Even "sinners" love those who love them *(Luke 6:32).*

Jill realized that not only did she have an opportunity to be obedient to what is taught in Scripture, but it was also a chance to reach out in love and kindness to a person who may be hurting.

Professional E-mail

Since so much work is done on the Internet these days, it's important to learn the right way to conduct communication via e-mail. Here are a few things we've found over the years that we think will help you.

Remember when responding to e-mail that there may be times you need to copy and paste the message you're referring to back into the message you're sending. Most e-mail programs have options that allow this to be done automatically. Sometimes an e-mail won't be read for hours or even days, and the person receiving it may have forgotten what the original e-mail said. We receive responses weeks after we send e-mail that say something like "Sounds great!" Nothing more, just a two-word reply. It's nice to get a reply, but if no other information is given, it's challenging to know to what they're referring to.

Also, be careful not to answer an e-mail with an abrupt response. You may be tempted to read an e-mail and then respond with "No, I don't want that" or another brusque answer. Keep in mind that there's not a conversation going on. When someone opens an e-mail and the first word is "no," it can set the stage for a negative feeling.

Never type in all capital letters—AND WE MEAN NEVER! It comes across as if you're shouting. Also, although you don't need to be perfect when sending e-mail, don't be too casual about your keyboarding skills. For example, something like this is ill-received: "i would like information on your services. please contact me asap. my number is 555-555-1234."

We sometimes get e-mail that looks like spam, and it's hard to determine whether to take the time to read it or just delete it.

If you're having a problem with a client, take a deep breath, and remember to respond kindly. If you act or react in anger, you could be wrong. If you allow yourself a reasonable amount of time, you can gauge the circumstances better. Wait, say a prayer, go do something else, and then get back to it. You'll be amazed at how much better things look when you do this.

> A gentle answer turns away wrath, but a harsh word stirs up anger *(Proverbs 15:1)*.

One growing trend with instant messages, Twitter messages, and e-mail coming at us relentlessly is responding to these while talking on the phone to someone else, whether that's a potential client, a client, or even a colleague. Avoid this. The person on the other end can hear that you're doing something else and will feel that his or her call isn't important enough to warrant a few minutes of your undivided attention. If you do need to answer an instant message, let the person you're speaking with on the phone know that you'll call back when you're finished, or ask him or her to hold while you finish your current task.

If your Internet service goes down and you can't respond to clients, call to let them know rather than leaving them waiting for work or an e-mail. Keep in mind that they often have clients who are relying on them also.

It's important to address the recipient of your e-mail with a proper greeting. "Hey there" is not a proper greeting. It's better to open with "Good morning" or "Good afternoon" when you send an e-mail response to someone you don't know on a personal level. If you know the person, by all means open up with a friendlier, more casual tone. Remember—that's the first thing the recipient will see when he or she opens your e-mail.

It is also important to close your e-mail in a professional tone. Those last few words just above your signature carry substantial weight. When you sign off, you want to leave the person feeling good about you and your company. Closing with "I look forward to talking with you soon," "Warmest regards," "Thanks," or "Hope you have an awesome day" makes the person feel valued and important to you. Try that as opposed to "Regards." Can you see the difference?

Be mindful of writing hurried e-mail. It can cost you sales if you don't look it over and think about how what you say will be received.

Also, be sure to include a signature line in each e-mail. Jill notes that she receives countless e-mails with no identification other than the e-mail address in the "from" field of the e-mail. Include your company name, title or position if applicable, web site address, and phone number. We often pull up an old e-mail to reconnect with someone. This is just one reason to include a phone number or at least a web site address.

In many e-mail programs such as Outlook, you can set different signature lines and choose which you would like to use for a particular e-mail. You can also set a default signature line that will apply to every e-mail you send unless you choose differently.

These are examples of signature lines we use:

Jill Hart
888-888-8888
CWAHM.com | CWAHD.com
See us in the *Wall Street Journal* [with link]

Diana Ennen
Author: *Virtual Assistant the Series & Workbook*
Virtual Word Publishing
http://www.virtualwordpublishing.com
888-888-8888

These signature lines leave the recipient with our names, phone numbers, and web site addresses so that the reader can easily contact us or take a look at our web sites.

Phone Etiquette

When talking to clients by phone, do your best to keep background noises to a minimum. Nothing shouts "unprofessional" like a television set blaring in the background or kids screaming. We know that's not always easy for work-at-home moms to pull off, but before making a phone call, think about what you can do to prevent background noise.

It might be best to wait and call later when things are quiet, or let the answering machine pick up an incoming call if the kids are rambunctious. Other options include getting a portable phone or cell phone and going into another room, stepping outside where it's quiet, or having an activity for the kids to do and a treat immediately following if they behave well.

Also consider other noises. Recently Diana was reminded that noises such as birds in the background can be disruptive to the conversation. "My birds happen to be like kids, and I do believe as soon as they know I'm on the phone, they get louder," she shares. Diana once recorded her segment for the CWAHM podcast, and when Jill edited it she could hear Diana's birds chirping in the background. While the sounds of birds chirping may be charming in person, it was very distracting in the background, and Diana had to re-record the entire segment.

Barking dogs are another distraction. Have you ever been talking on the phone with a client or potential client and had your dog go nuts over a squirrel in the yard? This can be avoided if you have a portable phone and take it to a quiet place to make your call.

Vacation and Time Off

It's crucial to let your clients know when you plan to take time off, even if it's just for a day or two. They count on your being there when they need to talk to you, and if they find out at the last minute that you're unavailable, it can cause them undue stress and perhaps cause them to miss a deadline. Give clients as much advance notice as possible if you're going to take time off, and as the time gets closer, send out a reminder e-mail.

You want to avoid your client getting an e-mail or a re-corded message along these lines: "Hi. Just wanted to let you know that I'm taking the next three days off but will be returning Wednesday evening. If you need anything, I'll be available then."

This may create a lot of stress for a client who had planned on sending you work that needed to be completed by Wednesday or Thursday. Because the client didn't know your plans, he or she couldn't plan ahead.

When planning a vacation or when you're on vacation, here are some tips that can help:

- Complete as many tasks as possible before leaving. Examples would be to send out a newsletter or finish client billing.

- Be disciplined about your time. Concentrate on exactly what needs to be done, and try to complete one task before moving on to the next one.

- Let your assistant help you. Tell her as soon as you know you're going on vacation that you'll need her during that time frame, so she can plan accordingly.

- If you're planning on taking the whole day off and don't need to answer e-mail, don't. You could receive an e-mail from a client who's in a panic or someone with a bad attitude who will spoil your day. Enjoy your day off, and come back renewed.

Diana had a recent incident that reinforced the no-e-mail-on-a-day-off rule. It was Easter time, and she was enjoying a fabulous time with her kids and family coloring eggs, making dinner and cookies, and doing Easter crafts.

She decided just to check through her e-mail, expecting to find electronic Easter cards. What she got instead was a note from one of her best clients saying they needed to cut down on her hours. Within minutes, the mood of the entire day changed, and unfortunately, she wasn't able to get it back. By Monday the client had a change of heart, but the damage had already been done. Diana's day off was overshadowed by that one e-mail. Maybe you can relate to her experience and have had a similar one. Remedy that by turning off the computer and stepping away—far, far away.

Ethical Work Habits

It's important in running a Christian work-at-home business that you're ethical in every way. If you're just starting out, you probably think an ethical dilemma couldn't happen to you, but down the road something may come up that will test you.

Prepare now by setting standards for your business early on. You want people to know and respect you, and you want to feel confident that you're doing the right thing.

Diana shared an experience in her business that can serve as an example of the importance of business ethics. It may mean turning down money—and it might be money you need—but you must be committed to doing the right thing.

Diana does press releases, and she had a client who wanted one written. The first thing the potential client sent was a link to the web site of a competing business. To make a long story short, Diana soon learned that her client was very close to copying his competitor's entire idea, including the web site. The client even sent Diana a link to one of the competitor's press

CLIENT RELATIONS

releases and told her to use that as a guide for writing the press release. In fact, his exact words were "Just change the name and a few things, and use this release."

Needless to say, Diana declined. Sure, she could have used the money, but she didn't want her business to be associated with another business that would take someone else's ideas and try to pass them off as their own. Diana values her reputation, so she declined the job. You'll feel good about your business and yourself if you hold yourself accountable to high ethical standards.

As business owners, we also must be aware when working online of the way we portray ourselves and our businesses on message boards and list-servers. No matter what industry you're in, you'll find that conflicts and disagreements abound online. There's a tendency to jump right on in and voice your opinion. Be aware that giving in to the temptation to throw in your two cents' worth can affect your professional standing. Think before you write. Is what you're writing beneficial to the conversation, or will it harm others? If this message is conveyed on another message board or to one of your clients, would it reflect badly on you? If it could be conceived as unkind or un-professional by any reader, don't post it.

Christians are called to be "light" in all arenas. When others bicker, you must stick to conversations that edify and build up others. Scripture tells us, "Do nothing out of selfish ambition or vain conceit, but in humility consider others better than yourselves" (Philippians 2:3).

It's very easy to lash out online, on a message board, or in an e-mail, but we must strive to be different from other voices online. This is what sets us apart, what draws people to work with us. They know they can ask questions without getting a rude response. They know they can trust you and that you're *different*. This is how our businesses become not only businesses but also our mission fields.

> He told them, "The harvest is plentiful, but the workers are few. Ask the Lord of the harvest, therefore, to send out workers into his harvest field" *(Luke 10:2)*.

Taking On Too Much?

Sometimes it's better to say no and decline a request for your services than to take on too much work. It's okay to be honest with your clients and say, "I'm booked now, but I should be able to have that back to you by [the projected date]." The client will let you know if that's acceptable. You don't know unless you ask. Also, if you're honest with clients, they appreciate it.

Here's an example. A client needs something done. You take on the assignment and tell him or her that you can have it done in two weeks. You're swamped and miss the deadline. The client is now upset and thinks you aren't professional and that you can't be trusted to do what you say you'll do.

Instead, it would be much better to tell the client that you're extremely busy right now but that you might be able to have the requested work back in three to four weeks. That works for you, it may work just fine for the client, and you won't have a disappointed or angry client. Clients will appreciate your honesty, and if you're able to complete the work in a shorter amount of time than you promised, you look even better.

In order to get the most done, make sure that your instructions from your clients are clear and that everyone understands what's involved.

Here are some tips to help lessen your load:

- Always write out instructions—you may even want to ask the customer to repeat the instructions back to you if you're speaking with him or her on the phone.

- When working with a client over the phone, always get his or her phone number first thing so that you can call back if you get disconnected. You may also need to call the client to follow up with some aspect of the job or order. Diana often prefers e-mail, because that provides a written account of what needs to be done. She often follows up a phone call with an e-mail verifying what was stated in the phone call.

- When questions arise, act promptly. Don't finish the entire project if you're unsure of any aspect of it. You don't want to spend precious time redoing the whole job because you misunderstood.

You may say to yourself, "My power and the strength of my hands have produced this wealth for me." But remember the LORD your God, for it is he who gives you the ability to produce wealth *(Deuteronomy 8:17-18)*.

8 FAMILY, FRIENDS, AND WORK

> Do nothing out of selfish ambition or vain conceit,
> but in humility consider others better than yourselves.
> Each of you should look not only to your own interests,
> but also to the interests of others *(Philippians 2:3-4).*

As Christians we know that we're to put others before ourselves. When we see a need, we try to reach out and do something to help. It's part of who we are and a core aspect of our character and relationship with God. Many times the reason we started a home-based business is to be at home for our children while helping to contribute financially.

One thing to be aware of in operating a home-based business, though, is that not everyone will understand your new career or the fact that you'll have business tasks to complete each day. Your time is precious, but many will assume that you can take on extra duties since you don't work a "real" nine-to-five job. You'll need to learn not to go overboard doing favors for family and friends that will use up time you should be working or could be spending with your family.

Diana has worked from home for almost twenty-five years. She has experienced it all, from helpful friends who give her a hand to those who think she has it easy as a work-at-home mom and try to pile on additional tasks.

In Diana's words, "I can't begin to tell you how many times I've been asked to watch a sick child because my friend didn't want to miss work. Or sometimes I'm asked if it's okay to send a child to my house after school for a couple of hours because *I don't work.*"

It took Diana a while to establish boundaries. When you start your business, have the rules in place on day one. If you don't, you'll have to go back and set boundaries, and that will be much more difficult than setting them from the start. Friends will hint that you're letting them down by changing the rules.

Also, keep in mind that the time you spend doing things for friends and family takes away from time with your family and your business. That isn't to say you can't occasionally help a friend in need, but be cautious of people who see you as a part-time babysitter or part-time help. You must protect yourself from the bitterness that will boil up if you allow others to take over your time.

You may also have friends and family who will take advantage of your business knowledge. It's a Christian mom's nature to enjoy helping others, but if you're not careful, helping others can turn into a major time commitment.

A recent example is a friend of Diana's who was starting a new business. It started with a few questions, which Diana was glad to answer. It turned into Diana's practically building her friend's business, offering web site ideas and bookkeeping basics, not to mention the five or ten e-mails every day, the phone ringing off the hook, and then every casual encounter turning into a business coaching session. Diana realized she needed to take charge and set some boundaries.

We're certainly not suggesting that you should not help others or that it's good to be stingy with your knowledge or resources. Learn what works for you and your business. If a friend asks for help, set up a time you can talk by phone or get together to discuss ways you can help. When you and your friend meet, be aware of what amount of time you can commit to helping her without shortchanging your family and your business.

> Each man should give what he has decided in his heart to give, not reluctantly or under compulsion, for God loves a cheerful giver (2 Corinthians 9:7).

Children add a whole new dimension to the workplace, especially when you work at home. Infants are fairly easy to work around—they sleep, you work. But as babies get older and need more interaction and constant monitoring, you'll be working two jobs—those of mom and business owner. The lines that separate the two can get very blurry at times, and it's important to be intentional in handling both.

There are a few different ways to go about being intentional in raising our children in the work-at-home environment. We try to do the majority of our work before our kids wake up in the morning, during naptime, and after bedtime. That isn't always possible, but we do our best.

Jill has also become involved with programs that take her and her kids out of the house. She says, "My daughter and I attended the MOPS (Mother of Preschoolers) group at our church when she was little. My son attended a 'Moms Day Out' program at a church in our area. He went to 'school,' as he called it, for two and a half hours each week. This gave him a structured program and interaction with other children his age. They did crafts and other activities. It helped build his self-confidence and independence, and I got time to work."

Many moms also find it possible to have a babysitter in their home during the day to help with the kids while they're focusing on their business. Another possible option is to trade babysitting days with a neighbor or friend who lives nearby. In some larger towns there are groups you can join and swap babysitting time.

If you choose to work your business full-time, it may become necessary to find someone to help you with the kids, the housework, or other tasks on a regular basis. Find the right balance, and it will be well worth the effort.

Keeping the Kids Entertained While You Work

Depending on the type of home-based work you do, working at home where your children are right there to be a part of things can be a wonderful part of the experience. However, there will be times your work demands peace and quiet, whether it's to make an important phone call, complete work to meet a deadline, or concentrate on the task at hand.

Below are six ways to keep your kids occupied when you need to be fully engaged in your work.

Naptime. Working while your child is taking a nap is an easy way to have the quiet you need for phone calls and other important tasks. If you have more than one child, try setting a specific time for them to nap each day, and they'll quickly adapt to the routine. Even thirty uninterrupted minutes a day can make a difference in your workload.

If you have older children who are home during the day, they, too, can observe some quiet time even if they don't necessarily sleep. It's good for children to have some time to themselves. They can play quietly in their room, read or color, or do another quiet activity. Keep in mind, though, that kids can be unpredictable. Have a backup plan ready for the days they won't nap or quietly entertain themselves.

Playtime. If your children are four years old or older, many times you can help them start an activity they can complete on their own. Put a small table near your desk, and allow them to play with Play Dough, work on a puzzle, or do a simple craft project. Take a break every so often to check their progress and help them if they need it. In fact, take a break as often as you can so they feel connected to you.

Older kids can sit at the kitchen table or somewhere else out of hearing range to do an activity or craft suitable for their age and interests.

Outdoor time. When the weather cooperates, send the kids outside for some fresh air. Be sure your children are old enough and mature enough to handle time outside by themselves. If you have a fenced back yard, that's probably the safest way. Another option is to buy outdoor activities that will keep your children occupied.

Consider if you can set up your office so that you can oversee a play area. Diana chose the family room for her office for that reason. It's connected to the patio, pool, and backyard. She can work and still keep an eye on everyone. One word of caution: if your home becomes the neighborhood hangout after school, it will quickly become stressful and noisy. Allowing your child to have a friend over might be nice, but four or five friends at the same time will try your nerves and bring on the gray hair.

Computer time. Allowing your children time on the computer can be a fun way for them to pass time quietly if you're on the phone or concentrating on other tasks. There are many educational web sites and games they can play online, such as SesameStreet.com, Noggin.com, PBSKids.org, and BigIdea.com.

Smaller children may also enjoy "typing." Open a blank document in your word processing program, and make the font large. As they get older, they'll become familiar with the letters and even learn to type their name and other words.

TV time. On the days your child is sick or it's too cold to play outside, consider allowing him or her to watch a movie or an allotted amount of television. Most children's movies are short enough to hold their attention and are also educational. Find movies or programs that meet your approval and adhere to your morals and beliefs.

Create an author. Give your children blank paper, and put their writings in a three-ring binder. Encourage them to write a "book" and share the adventures of the day, tell about their friends or their pets, or write about whatever else interests them. Keep colored pencils on hand, and encourage them to draw illustrations to go along with their writing. They can even design a cover for the books; then encourage them to read their writings that night after dinner. Also, make sure to keep copies of all these treasures. Every year you can see their skill level increasing.

Handling the Workload When the Kids Are Sick

One of the benefits of working at home is being there for your children when they're under the weather and can't go to school. Diana's daughter gained respect for what Diana does after a few days of being home sick. However, it can also cause you stress.

Here are some tips to help you both through these times:

- Preventative measures. Parents hope the kids won't get sick in the first place. To reduce sick time, provide kids with a healthful diet and plenty of exercise. Give them vitamins and plenty of vitamin C, and most important, keep them away from other sick children when possible. Remember—it's okay to be the bad guy and not let them play down the street if someone in that household has the flu.

- Have a laptop or spare computer available so you can continue to work and still be close by if you're needed.

- Have a backup plan. This is when you need an assistant you can call on. Yes, you probably won't make as much money that day, but an assistant can keep the business running for you.

- When your kids are sick, don't stress. Realize that you'll be able to get your work done once they're well and back in school. When necessary, fill your clients in so they understand and can be prepared for any delays. Diana handles this by not worrying her clients if her workload is manageable even with a sick child at home. However, if she knows she's going to fall behind, she lets her clients know as soon as possible so they can prioritize the work they've given her and she can complete the most important tasks.

- Keep them occupied. We keep backup activities from Christmas or simple crafts around that our kids can do as they begin feeling better. They get so bored when they're sick, but if you have something special for them to do, it helps tremendously. Those after-Christmas sales can bring hours of enjoyment at a fraction of the cost.

- Enjoy the special time with your kids. This is one of the blessings of working at home. We feel closer to our kids each time we have this extra time with them, and they love knowing that Mom is there for them.

Snow Days

The words *snow day* always bring a smile to children's faces, but to work-at-home moms it often means unexpected complications. However, it *is* possible to enjoy a snow day and get work done as well. Right, Jill?

Whenever possible, take a few hours out of your day to enjoy your kids. Especially if your children are in school full-time, this can be time spent making precious memories with them.

For example, one year Jill and her kids were stuck inside for three days while almost two feet of snow fell outside. Her husband was out of town for the week on a business trip, so she was on her own to find a way to work around the situation. Jill decided that each afternoon the kids, who were one and five at the time, would have "learning time" while she worked. She set the kids up with activities appropriate for their ages, and they had a blast. The kids felt as if they were doing something special, because they were playing on the computer and coloring on printer paper, and Jill was able to work while still keeping an eye on them. Snow days call for moms to use their imaginations.

Behold, children are a gift of the LORD (Psalm 127:3, NASB).

Taking Care of Number Two—Your Spouse

We realize it's just as important to nurture our relationships with our husbands as it is to nurture our relationships with our kids and our business relationships.

Don't forget to spend important one-on-one time with your husband. It's easy when starting a business to get used to working every night, and sometimes it's a necessity. However, remember that one of your objectives is to focus on prioritizing your time so that your whole family wins.

We've found ways to give adequate time to our business and our families. For example, Diana needed to be able to answer e-mail in the evening, so she bought a used laptop and was able to answer e-mail while she watched TV at the same time. For a long while she also had a spare computer set up in the living room. That was ideal.

Diana sometimes needed to work in the evenings because one of her children was sick and she was busy caring for that child during the day. When asked about what her mother does, the first thing Diana's daughter, Amber, always said was "She works at home so when I'm sick I can stay home." Diana thinks it's very possible that Amber took advantage of that set-up a time or two.

Each family will have its own circumstances to work around. Some husbands watch the kids while Mom works in the evening. Just like everything else, remember that communication is key, and keeping to a schedule is also important. Communicate with your husband, and figure out what works best for him, for you, and for your family. Two of the goals of your business are to have a happy, healthy family as well as to achieve success in your business.

Tell Your Husband How He Can Help You

Husbands play a part in the success of their wife's home-based business. Here are six ways your husband can help ensure your home runs smoothly and that you are successful in your home-based business. Share these six tips with your husband. He won't know if you don't tell him:

1. **Encouragement is key.** Sometimes all your wife needs in order to be successful with whatever she is working on is a little encouragement. Most of the time she will not be surrounded by other adults cheering her on. Often a simple "I know you can do it" from you is just what she needs.

2. **Help with whatever she's doing.** Depending on the business, there are helpful things you can do to lighten her load. Jill's husband often helps with the web site, or if she needs someone to write a script, he sets up an e-mail account or proofreads a document. Some of the tasks aren't going to be the most glamorous, but five minutes could save your partner hours. Diana's husband is instrumental in keeping all the computers working and the equipment in tip-top shape.

3. **Watch the kids.** Your wife is at home with the kids all day every day. Sometimes she needs some time to work without distractions. If the kids are constantly asking questions and bugging your wife, she can't get anything done.

4. **Listen.** Your wife might not have a large support system or other coworkers to bounce ideas off. You can be there for her to talk to and, more important, to listen to the ideas she has. This goes hand in hand with encouragement. Listen and offer encouragement.

5. **Let her run the show.** This is her business, and she gets to call the shots. Jill runs all her "big" ideas

past him, because she trusts his abilities and business sense, but the day-to-day running of the business is her responsibility, and she makes those decisions.

6. **Pray.** Never underestimate the power of prayer. Pray for your wife and her business, and pray for wisdom and insights into ways you can help her.

By following these six simple tips, you can help strengthen your wife's home-based business. She'll appreciate your efforts, and your marriage will benefit as well. Supporting your work-at-home wife is one of the best ways to show you care.

Work-at-Home Fashion Tips

Diana has been working at home since 1985 and loves it. However, she recently discovered she was in a work-at-home fashion rut. Here's her story:

I live in south Florida, so most days it's Capri pants and short-sleeve tops. On Fridays it's shorts and tops. Of course, when I go out and visit clients or attend networking events, I dress more professionally. But with more and more virtual networking, that's happening less and less.

When I took on a new client last year, Jamie Yasko-Mangum, author of *Look Speak and Behave: Expert Advice on Image, Etiquette, and Effective Communication for the Professional,* I was reminded of how fun it is to dress up. I began making changes to my wardrobe and to my daily routine. What an amazing difference! I'm more productive and much more creative. Just getting dressed for success *does* make a difference. Even when no one else sees me, I feel more confident, and it shows in my work. I encourage you to try it. Even baby steps help. Comfort is a major factor for me, so I had to find clothes that looked good and also felt good.

I also discovered what an amazing difference a pair of "heels" makes. Okay, confess. When was the last time you put on heels for work? Be honest. I couldn't remember the last time. I always wear shoes, but they're sandals. I challenge you to put on a pair of heels. I found that I want to get out and network more; I want to talk on the phone more; I want to write more. Try it!

Get dressed for work every day, put on makeup every day, and wear those heels occasionally. You'll be amazed at the difference it makes.

9 STAYING MOTIVATED

You'll likely start off in your new job or business as a gung-ho, success-minded work-at-home mom. Six months or a year later, though, things may seem a little less exciting. You'll be sitting in your home office with piles of work to do, the phone ringing off the hook, laundry going, dishes piled in the sink, kids in the next room fighting, and the dog eating your latest project. Will you be able to hang in there and keep yourself motivated? What does it take to make it in this crazy work-at-home world?

There are ways you can keep yourself motivated. One motivating factor is to know that you're where God wants you. Here are Jill's thoughts:

> As I look back, I can see how He placed all the steps in order. I thought I was in control of this whole process. No way. God gave me the desires of my heart. I didn't even know what my desires were, but since He's the one who placed those desires in me, He knew perfectly.

> The most important thing to remember is that God will be there for you no matter how impossible things might feel at times. There have been days I was ready to just throw in the towel—things weren't going as well as I hoped, I felt guilty about working while my daughter was around, the task seemed too much, and the excuses went on and on. During this time God gently reminded me that many moms don't have the opportunities He has given me. It's a gift from God to be at home with my children, raising them to follow His ways.

Psalm 37:4 says, "Delight yourself in the LORD and he will give you the desires of your heart." Focus your heart on Him, and let Him guide you.

We can glorify God through our businesses. Many times God has taken us through tough experiences and then used those experiences to minister to other Christian work-at-home moms. Jill recently received a call from a CWAHM who was interested in advertising on Jill's web site. Early in the phone conversation, the woman broke down into tears, explaining that she was desperate to get her business going because her husband was very ill. She was spent emotionally, and she and Jill talked for quite a while about finding comfort in Christ. God took that conversation from a business transaction to a very personal conversation between two members of His family.

We're so honored when God allows us to be a part of the work that He's doing. We believe that nothing happens by accident. It was no accident that this woman ran across CWAHM. com, and it was not an accident that she called that day. God is in control, and He uses us despite ourselves.

Jill states, "Another thing that has helped motivate me is learning to fully trust God. He's teaching me daily that it *is* worth it to tough it out and work from home—even though at times it can be very stressful. It's amazing how God gives us a passion for something and then allows that to be the very thing we get to do each day. When I think of how God has blessed my life through CWAHM.com, I'm overwhelmed with thankfulness."

It's also important to be mindful of the Proverbs 31 woman. She shows us a picture of a woman who runs her home and also works from home. She provides food, purchases land, and makes profitable trades. Read Proverbs 31, and take careful notes of all this "noble woman" accomplishes and is responsible for. She must be passionate about her family to do everything she does every day.

You may have days when you become fearful that you won't succeed. If that happens, rely on what God says about fear. "God did not give us a spirit of timidity, but a spirit of power, of love and of self-discipline" (2 Timothy 1:7). God has given you everything you need to conquer fear. You can rely on Him and believe that He's in control. He'll see you through.

"In all things God works for the good of those who love him" (Romans 8:28).

Take your doubts and fears to Him through prayer. He already knows what you're thinking and feeling anyway, but just expressing it to Him can help. If possible, ask your spouse or a good friend to become a prayer partner—someone you can talk with through tough times and with whom you can share prayer requests and praises.

Be in constant prayer. Lay your business and your fears at His feet. Prayer will help you look at life from His perspective.

As you set out on your work-at-home adventure, recognize that it can take some time for your business to be financially successful. If you're aware of this at the start and plan accordingly, you're already one step ahead of the game and won't become unduly discouraged.

Be aware also that the timeframe for a business to be financially successful depends in large part on the type of business you're establishing. Jill was a representative with Southern Living at Home for a short time and was able to hold some parties and see an income right away. In cases like this, you must focus on maintaining this income to keep it successful. When Diana started her word processing business, she was also able to gain clients immediately. However, when Jill began her web site, it took longer to develop her client and advertising base.

Finding Success

Two necessary ingredients to running your own home-based business are creativity and persistence.

Be creative in how you market your products or services. Start by thinking of ways you can reach customers by standing out from others offering similar products. Design contests and free offers, and research other marketing strategies that will bring customers to your web site. Try to determine what your customers are looking for once they reach your web site, and offer the most popular products on your front page. Keep in mind that your web site must be fresh, so consider changing the items or text on your site's front page often. This will continue to pique the interest of your customers each time they visit, and it encourages them to keep coming back.

Develop persistence. Don't start out strong, marketing yourself in every way possible, and then simply stop marketing. Most profitable businesses must market continually to keep their business successful. Can you think of a single successful business that does no advertising? It's unlikely that you'll be able to just sit back and let the sales roll in from your web site. Not really. Business just doesn't work that way. We've found that on Christian Work at Home Moms (CWAHM.com) the businesses that achieve the most success are the consistent advertisers, the ones that advertise regularly and keep their businesses, banners, and other promotions in front of their potential clients.

This doesn't mean you must spend hundreds of dollars each month to advertise your home-based business. It does mean that you must be persistent in the advertising that you choose to do. Budget your advertising dollars so that you can do a small amount of consistent advertising. Get involved in groups online, and ask advice from other successful moms. Whatever you do, don't stop talking about your business.

Most important, don't give up. *Success is possible.* Take the time to be creative in marketing your business, be persistent, and don't expect profits immediately. Set realistic goals for your business, and be patient while your business grows into something you can be proud of. Soon you'll be among the millions of work-at-home moms who are enjoying it all: being home with the kids, realizing financial freedom, and basking in the pride of having their own home-based business.

It's important in your home business to have your "moment in time." Go out and find a song that inspires you. Celebrate often. At the Ennen household, every single accomplishment is celebrated with family and friends. Diana believes that's one of the reasons her kids love her businesses so much—they're constantly celebrating. Don't wait for the big accomplishments. Celebrate each small one *now.*

❈ ❈ ❈

We hope you'll enjoy reading the following stories of a few women who have been successful with their home-based businesses.

After I had my first daughter twelve years ago, I decided that I did not want to go back to work. I didn't do a lot of preplanning, although I don't recommend that.

I began doing freelance work in public relations and marketing, and within about six months I was desperately looking for other moms to network with so that I could learn from them, ask questions, and find out how they were being successful with their home-based businesses. That's what gave me the idea for Home-Based Working Moms (HBWM), which I started in 1995 when my little girl was four or five months old. I devote myself to HBWM now and have given up freelance work.

HBWM is similar to a chamber of commerce except that it's made up of moms from across the country who network through the Internet. When a mom joins, she gets t-shirt and a bumper sticker and begins receiving a monthly print newsletter and an e-newsletter, becomes part of an e-mail discussion group, and enjoys other perks.

I love working at home. It makes me feel there's more balance in my life. Even if I didn't need to work, I would want to, because I enjoy the creativity, and it gives me an outlet and a way to connect with other moms in addition to fulfilling my role as a mother. I love being a mom, but I also love using my gifts and talents in a business setting.

We recently launched Hire My Mom, <www.hiremy mom.com>. I came up with the idea for HireMyMom.com a couple years ago, but I knew it wasn't the right time to start it. I was passionate about beginning the business, because there are so many women who want to work and are really good at what they do, but they also want to be available to their children more than going to an office or workplace every day would allow. The goal of Hire My Mom is to market these talented mom professionals to businesses who want to out-source work.

There are 5.4 million moms who put their careers on hold to be at home with their children. A lot of them want to work ten, fifteen, or twenty hours a week to bring in a little extra money while they enjoy those years of motherhood. I'm glad to be able to help.

—Lesley Spencer-Pyle
Founder of Hire My Mom and
Home-Based Working Moms

* * *

As far back as I can remember, I've wanted to be a secretary. After I graduated from high school in 1971, my first job was as a secretary to the engineering department at a major astronautics company in southern California. Nearly twenty years later, I decided to leave the corporate world and headed out to start my own secretarial and résumé service.

When I opened Fastype in 1991, there was no Internet. Because no one wanted to travel very far to get a letter typed or a brochure typeset, we were relegated to serving local clients only. I lived in a small rural area, and my typical clients were small, family-owned businesses, organizations, and individuals needing word processing and desktop publishing, as well as a little transcription and a few résumés here and there. When the Internet came into play, it was a whole new ballgame. With web sites, e-mail, and everything the Internet offers, technology exploded, and the geographical locale of clients was no longer an issue.

Once my web site was up and running and things started to settle down and fall into place, I started seeing a pattern in the types of things I enjoyed doing most and the types of clients I was attracting—professional speakers and business and life coaches. I started marketing more specifically to that niche. Professional speakers and business and life coaches became my target market.

It's exciting work. Speakers and business and life coaches are always on the go and always producing a new product or starting a new venture. Along with their need for general services, they also need more specialized services. Every day provides new challenges, and that keeps my job fresh and varied.

Not all virtual assistants enjoy doing the same things, and not all virtual assistants serve the same niche market. One of the things I love most about being in business for myself is that I can choose the type of work I do and the clients I work for. I recommend finding out what you're good at and what you enjoy—then get to work.

—*Terry L. Green*
Master Virtual Assistant
<http://www.myfastype.com>

✳ ✳ ✳

I've been a single mom for more than six years, and I've missed out on so many things in my son's life. He had spent most of his life going to daycare, and I finally decided enough was enough—I was ready to embark on a career that allowed me to work at home, even though

I wasn't sure where or how to start. I found my answer when my friend Kelly McCausey of WAHM Talk Radio (<http://www.wahmtalkradio.com>) asked me if I would be interested in becoming her virtual assistant. I had never even heard of a virtual assistant before, but I was eager to find a career that would give me the opportunity to be at home with my son.

Kelly took me under her wing, and in just a few months I was growing my client list and was able to leave my job and start my own at-home business. I provide fast, efficient, and excellent work. As I provide excellent service to my clients, word gets around, and that's how I've grown my clientele. My clients are satisfied with the job I do, and my business continues to become more and more successful.

—*Tishia Lee*
Virtual Assistant
<*http://www.tishiasavestime.com*>

✳ ✳ ✳

I've had a home business since 1999 with a company called Reliv International. I had no idea what network marketing was until I got involved with Reliv. I had no intentions of starting a business—I just wanted the products. I have Crohn's disease, Sjogren's syndrome, Grave's disease, and interstitial cystitis and was making a last-ditch effort to find something to help me feel better. The Reliv products were an answer to prayer. After a few months of taking the products, I started noticing some improvement. It was enough to keep me on the product and take a look at the business. After six months, I was seeing some life-changing health results. I checked Reliv out very thoroughly and decided to try out a home business.

My original reason for starting my business was to help other people feel better using the products. After a few months in the business, I realized that I was actually making money. I didn't know many people who actually made money in home businesses. I decided to take Reliv more seriously and treat it like a business. My checks started to grow, and I was able to leave my corporate job of five years as a bookkeeper/office manager. Because of the time freedom that Reliv allowed me, I was able to work part time for a Christian theatre group. What a blessing to be able to help out a Christian ministry!

At this point our Reliv business had exceeded all my expectations. I was working from home and giving my time to a Christian ministry, my health had improved so much that I was functioning at a "normal" level, and I was working with a company that had a mission to "nourish the world." It was then that God revealed the most important reason for giving me Reliv—I became pregnant after seven years of infertility. We had been only two days away from completing our adoption paperwork. It was a miracle.

We were very scared and excited at the same time. My health problems could cause potential harm to the baby. Although I felt good, there were still major concerns for the health of the baby, and it was a very rocky pregnancy. I took the Reliv products as my prenatal nutrition. I thank God for giving me the gift of Reliv five years earlier to get my body ready for this pregnancy. The nutrition in the products kept both me and our baby healthy. Our little miracle—Sammy—was born five weeks early. He was five pounds, three ounces, and very healthy.

God blessed us with a business that helps others with their health and finances. God gave me the most important job on earth: being a mother. I take that job very seriously.

—*Karen Range*

<http://relivforhealth.org/wahoo.htm>

❀ ❀ ❀

I'm amazed when I look back to my life three years ago. I took on a large amount of debt with a business that was not a good fit for me. I was under stress and getting far from God. I believed that I could be successful at anything I tried. The problem was—I did it without God. I pushed Him aside to try to prove that I could do it alone.

Then I was introduced to a company with a product I loved, but this time I did things differently. I discussed it with my husband and prayed about it, asking God for a clear answer about starting a new business. I decided that it had to be a family business, meaning my kids would work with me rather than watch me. For the past two years, God has been so faithful. My husband and children are working with me to build a thriving business that gives me the opportunity to bless so many people through the Internet and beyond. I gave it to God, and He gave back—tenfold!

—*Kelly Wissink*

<http://www.soyandbeyond.com>

✳ ✳ ✳

Through my web site I provide visitors with a resource to find free birthday treats offered by local companies. People can go to <www.freebirthdaytreats.com> and browse through the listings for the treats that appeal to them instead of spending hours trying to locate great offers on their own. In addition, there's information for birthday discounts, gift ideas, birthday supplies and services, and even funny birthday videos.

It was a completely random idea, but it blossomed and took on a life of its own. I'm a bargain hunter, and I love sharing my great finds with others. About a year ago I was sharing one of my bargains with a few friends—a wonderful steak-and-lobster dinner that I had received as a free birthday treat from a local steakhouse—and they all wanted to know how to get on the mailing list for their birthdays. I did some online research to determine if there were sites that provided this kind of information, and I found a few. But my idea had a few variations from what I found online, so I decided to go for it.

The three main traits that are important in a person who wants to start a business are patience, persistence, and the willingness to learn. My business is mostly computer-based, although to support the services on the web site I sell ad space. So I have to be willing to call companies and solicit sales.

One of the things I love most about my business is that I meet so many great people. It's amazing how my life has changed since I started on this path. I've been blessed by the number of people who have offered to help me and have continued to support and encourage me.

My suggestion for women who want to start a business at home is to make a list of the things you do that bring joy to your life—or things you would *like* to do. Then see if there are ways you might possibly start a business related to that favorite thing.

Stick to a business schedule and a family schedule. For instance, I don't even try to work on weekday mornings while the kids are getting ready for school, and I try not to work from 3:15 P.M. to 8:30 P.M. Although I've been known to sneak into my office on a weekend, I make an effort to keep weekends free for family time.

—*Julie Northrop*
<www.freebirthdaytreats.com>

In closing, we pray that this book will be a blessing to you and will guide you in your search for a work-at-home career. Please visit our web sites at <http://www.cwahm.com> and <http://www.virtualwordpublishing.com>. You may also e-mail Jill at <jill@cwahm.com> and Diana at <diana@virtualwordpublishing.com>.

May God provide you strength and encouragement as you begin your work-at-home journey, and may it be a blessing for years to come.

ABOUT THE AUTHORS

Jill Hart is the founder of Christian Work at Home Moms, CWAHM.com. Jill has worked from home since 2000 and started her own home-based business to assist other Christians who desire to work from home while maintaining a godly life. Jill and her husband, Allen, of CWAHD.com (Christian Work at Home Dads), reside in Nebraska with their two children.

Jill's articles can be found across the Internet, and her articles have been featured on web sites such as drlaura.com and clubmom.com, and she's an author on ezinearticles.com. Jill is a contributing author in *Laundry Tales, The Business Mom Guide Book, I'll Be Home for Christmas,* and *Faith Deployed: Daily Encouragement for Military Wives.*

Diana Ennen

Diana Ennen is the author of numerous books, including *Virtual Assistant—The Series: Become a Highly Successful, Sought After VA* (<http://www.va-theseries.com>) and the accompanying workbook, *Words from Home: Start, Run and Profit from a Home-Based Word Processing Business;* and the *Home Office Recovery Plan.* She's the president of Virtual Word Publishing (<http://www.virtualwordpublishing.com>) and provides publicity and marketing advice to clients as well as start-up advice for virtual assistants and home-based businesses. She may reached by e-mail at <diana@virtualwordpublishing.com> or via her web site at <www.virtualwordpublishing.com>.